HOW TO DRAW PLANTS

The techniques of botanical illustration

KEITH WEST

Foreword by Wilfrid Blunt

TIMBER PRESS
in association with
The British Museum (Natural History)

Published in North America in 1996 by
Timber Press, Inc.
The Haseltine Building
133 S.W. Second Avenue, Suite 450
Portland, Oregon 97204, U.S.A.
1–800–327–5680 (U.S.A. & Canada only)

Reprinted 1997, 1998, 1999, 2000, 2001, 2002

ISBN 0–88192–350–8

Designed by Pauline Harrison
Printed in Hong Kong / China

FRONTISPIECE Creeping buttercup,
Ranunculus reperus. Pencil, continuous tone.

Contents

Acknowledgements 6

Foreword by Wilfrid Blunt 7

Introduction 9

1 The past 12

2 Basic equipment 21

3 Concepts 25

4 Plant handling 27

5 Plants in detail 33

6 Pencil 64

7 Ink 78

8 Scraper board 92

9 Water-colour and gouache 98

10 Acrylics 127

11 Photography 140

12 Preparing for the printer 144

Glossary 146

Selected bibliography 149

Index 150

Acknowledgements

I would like to thank Mr John Cannon and Mr Robert Cross, British Museum (Natural History), for encouragement from the beginning – and the former for critically reading the text and for helpful suggestions; Mrs Brenda Herbert, Thĕ Herbert Press, for her sensitive editing; and Mrs Judith Diment, British Museum (Natural History), for professional advice about the bibliography and for her help in selecting illustrations from the Museum's archives.

For permission to use illustrations I would like to thank the following: the Graphische Sammlung Albertina, Vienna (fig. 1); the British Museum (Natural History) (figs 2–8 and pp. 105–108); Mary Grierson and The Bentham-Moxon Trust, Royal Botanic Gardens, Kew (fig. 9); Anne Ophelia Dowden and Harper & Row, Publishers, Inc. (fig. 10); Department of Lands and Survey, New Zealand (frontispiece and figs 54–6); Stella Ross-Craig and Bell & Hyman (fig. 58); Dr Peter H. Raven, Director, Missouri Botanical Garden, USA (fig. 65); and Botany Division, Department of Scientific and Industrial Research, New Zealand (fig. 72 and p. 118, top).

With the exception of figs 1–10, 58 and the colour plates on pp. 105–108, all illustrations are by the author.

Foreword

Over the past thirty years there has been a tremendous revival of interest in the drawing and painting of flowers by amateurs. Some of these artists, though frankly admitting small knowledge of botany, have managed to produce extremely accurate portraits of plants; others have been content to discover an absorbing hobby which affords them the same satisfaction that this occupation gave to Victorian maidens combatting boredom in remote country houses. Given reasonable eyesight and a tolerably steady hand, the drawing of plants can be pursued into oldest age, and I recall with pleasure the pride with which an old lady in Bath showed me a bunch of anemones that she had painted – and none too badly – on her hundredth birthday!

Yet, inexplicably, to the best of my knowledge there has never until now been a really *thorough* book supplying the answers to all those technical questions that I am still constantly being asked by people wishing to take up botanical illustration, either professionally or as a hobby: 'What pencils, what pens, what inks do you recommend?', 'How do you "fix" a drawing?', 'What papers are best for watercolour painting?', 'How does one handle acrylics?' – and a hundred others. So it was with eager anticipation that I learned that that admirable botanical artist, Keith West, had produced what promised to be exactly what was required, and when I received a copy of the typescript and was asked if I would write a foreword, I realized at once that here, at long last, was just what we had all been waiting for.

The book is, perhaps, primarily directed at the would-be professional, but the bulk of it also gives invaluable help to even the most humble and struggling amateur. Would that I myself had had access to such a mine of information when, many years ago now, I too was striving, unaided, to draw and paint flowers!

In short, Keith West's timely book cannot be too highly recommended, and I hope it will have the great success that it undoubtedly deserves.

Wilfrid Blunt

For Margaret

Introduction

This book is intended as a guide for those who would like to portray plants with regard for botanical detail. I hope that it will help not only those whose aim is to provide plates for the scientific press with its disciplined requirements, but also students aiming to become artists and illustrators partly or wholly devoted to botanical topics, amateur and professional botanists wishing to illustrate their own works, artists looking for an extension of their range, and those with a keen but less focused interest in art and natural history who want to record accurately flowers that have given them pleasure.

Detailed botanical portraits intended for publication are generally referred to as 'illustrations', a word sometimes used pejoratively as if 'illustration' should inevitably be placed in a lower category than 'art'. Though many plant illustrations inform while possessing little or no aesthetic content, there are others which, in spite of the constraints imposed by the format of the printed page and the requirements of an author, have been long accepted as works of art. The splendid work of Dürer's, 'Das Grosse Rasenstück' (fig. 1) remains splendid whether it is thought of as fine art, illustration, or the first ecological study. In this book 'illustrator' and 'artist' are therefore used for the most part without hierarchical intent.

Books of general botanical interest are now often illustrated by photographs. This may be no bad thing for the artist in that anything that promotes botany to the public is in the long term likely to provide more creative opportunities – and ultimately the whole study of botany rests upon public support. Superficially it might appear that the artist and the photographer are in competition; sometimes they are, but there are limitations to each endeavour, and where these are recognized the strengths of each may be exploited. Given the great variety of plant life, to say nothing of the diversity of ability in illustrators and photographers, there would be little sense in trying to generalize here about one form of illustration versus the other. Nevertheless the finest works of the botanical artist have an individual character and style not to be seen in acres of photographs.

The artist can often interpret in a way that is beyond the capacity of the camera; for example, certain characters such as hair-type and pigment may have much greater botanical relevance in some groups than others, and the illustrator can reflect this significance. This view is supported by George H. M. Lawrence in his *Taxonomy of Vascular Plants*: '... in the photographic rendition the features of particular structures often are obscured by less relevant aspects – as vesture or overlapping parts, features readily de-emphasized in the line drawing. There is little question but that a well and accurately executed drawing is superior to and more satisfactory than the best photographic reproduction.'

1 Albrecht Dürer *Das grosse Rasenstück* (1503)

Currently the main media used for botanical illustration are those described in the following chapters, but this is not to slight the excellent productions of those who happen to work in other ways. A catalogue of a recent International Exhibition of Botanical Art and Illustration held at the Hunt Institute (see p. 20) reveals artists using the following means of expression in addition to those discussed here: woodcuts and wood engravings; lead cuts; copper and steel engravings; dry point; etchings; lithographs; serigraphs; aquarelle pencil; colour pencil; crayon; pen and wash; oils; and egg tempera. Lino cuts are also featured, though, as might be expected, these appear more concerned with broad decorative elements than with accuracy of detail.

The past year or so has seen the introduction of alkyd resin paints in which the pigments are bound by oil-modified synthetic resins instead of linseed oil. No doubt these paints, and other new products, will also find their way into the armoury of the botanical artist. So far there is no medium that suits all tastes and all purposes; each is limited. These limitations provide part of the stimulus: without the constant striving to overcome deficiencies in skill, the complexity of the subject and the disadvantages of the chosen medium, there would be small satisfaction in success.

You should be cautioned about cutting plants and, more seriously, about digging them up. In some countries and in some areas, particularly with common species, little harm is done, but it is important to know the conservation status of the plant and the legal position before taking plant material. Even though as illustrator you may be assisting in a scientific inquiry, this will not excuse decimation of a rare plant population. The end results are the same whether plants are gathered with scientific aims in mind or for the most frivolous reasons.

Anyone long employed in illustrating plants can scarcely fail to develop an appreciation that may in some approach nature-worship. Goethe and Ruskin, for instance, drew plants as a means of getting to know them better. The latter wrote of flowers, 'It is difficult to give them the accuracy of attention necessary to see their beauty without drawing them.' (*Proserpina*, 1874–86.) This view has doubtless been echoed by others, including scientists who have found that the 'accuracy of attention' needed to depict a plant's parts is also a path to knowledge. Ruskin's aim was to 'see their beauty' and he seems largely to have been exasperated or even disgusted by scientific interest; at the other extreme there are botanists who flinch at an aesthetic emphasis – a scan through a recently published study describing numerous species, many of which happen to be cultivated for their loveliness, discloses the one epithet 'showy', used in a single instance.

I feel confident that most, if not all, botanical artists would join me in saying that *all* plants can be brought to yield artistic and intellectual pleasure – some in great bounty, others sparingly. I have not yet found a plant that completely lacked rewards for the searching mind and eye. This is not to say that the illustrator's life is all sweetness and light – some species are so complex in form that they test the resolve of even the lionhearted; and financial gains are modest. Yet the botanical artist may be envied – each day is spent absorbingly, skills are challenged, tangible results are produced that are pleasing to most and harmful to none, the work neither pollutes nor guzzles the earth's resources. The aim is *to illuminate*, in the sense both of *to enlighten* and *to adorn*, and success is measured by the extent to which this is achieved.

1 The past

Botanical art dates from the roots of civilization. Though the first known gropings in art are largely concerned with hunting, early man did leave a few traces of his awareness of plants. And by 1500 BC, in the Great Temple of Thutmose III at Karnak, a sophisticated appreciation of plant life was reflected in a realistic stone relief figuring some 275 species.

From this promising beginning little more than fragments remain, until curiosity about the medicinal properties of plants led to the production of the first illustrated herbals by, among others, Krateuas the physician. Such works were described by Pliny the Elder in the first century AD, but unfortunately the prototypes are lost and, instead of building upon this classical foundation, workers copied the original illustrations again and again. The copies themselves were copied and at each remove small misrepresentations accrued until plates often passed beyond the point where they could be clearly related to particular species, or even in extreme cases to any portion of the plant kingdom.

It was not until the Renaissance that the arts again returned to naturalism and this movement was also to be seen in the portrayal of flowers. Though plants were mostly used as embellishments in larger compositions, a few separate studies are known from artists such as Bellini, Pisanello, da Vinci, and Dürer. The artistic climate of this period, coupled with the means of reproduction available from the woodcut, made possible the refined illustrations of Brunfels' *Herbarum Vivae Eicones* published in Strasbourg in 1530. It is from this work that scientific botanical illustration is said to date. Further advances were made in the publications of Fuchs a few years later, and of his immediate successors.

The texts of Brunfels and Fuchs were derived from earlier writers. Their main merit lies in the inclusion of accurate and lovely woodcuts made from *living* models. Ironically, although the names of Brunfels and Fuchs have long been honoured, their artists, respectively Hans Weiditz and Albrecht Meyer, remain obscure.

2 Hans Weiditz *Convallaria majalis* L. from *Contrafayt Kreüterbuch* . . . Strasszburg, 1532–37

With growing botanical knowledge came greater demands upon illustrators for yet finer detail than was obtainable from the woodcut (it was not until the nineteenth century that the virtuosi of the wood engraving flourished). At the close of the sixteenth century the copper plate provided for these new requirements by permitting minute structures to be recorded and printed.

The development of travel in the seventeenth century led to countless opportunities for artists working both overseas and in the many gardens, founded about this time, ablaze with new introductions from abroad. Horticulture joined botany and medicine as an outlet for plant artists.

The binomial system of classification evolved by Linnaeus in the eighteenth century, together with fervid botanical exploration, introduced a golden age of magnificent botanical art which persisted well into the next century. At this time Georg Ehret found favour with noble patrons in England, and Gerard van Spaëndonck and Pierre-Joseph Redouté worked in Paris. Through modern printing techniques the paintings of the latter artist are if anything more widely known now than in his own day; particularly the plates of *Les Roses*. This wave of talent peaked with the achievements of two brothers born near Vienna, Franz and Ferdinand Bauer. Their lives make a strange contrast. Though he worked mainly in England, Ferdinand travelled widely, even voyaging to Australia with Matthew Flinders, while Franz, on reaching Kew in his thirty-second year in 1790, stayed there contentedly until his death fifty years later.

It was in 1787 that the *Botanical Magazine*, still flourishing today, was founded by William Curtis. This journal has through almost 200 years provided support for a roll-call of notable artists. An intriguing curiosity is that from its inception until February 1948 (but for the 1921 volume) all the printed plates were hand-coloured.

With a swelling interest in botany during the eighteenth and nineteenth

BELOW LEFT
3 Georg Dionysius Ehret (1708–70) *Iberis semper-florens* L.

BELOW RIGHT
4 Gerard van Spaëndonck (1746–1822) *Solanum macrocarpon* L.

Gesse à larges feuilles.   *Latyrus latifolius*

5 Pierre-Joseph Redouté
(1759-1840) *Latyrus latifolius*
L. from *Choix des plus belles
fleurs et des plus beaux fruits*
by P.-J. Redouté, Paris,
1827-33

OPPOSITE
6 Franz Andreas Bauer
(1758-1840) *Epipactus
palustris* (L.) Crantz

centuries, many countries produced their first illustrated Floras. This en-
thusiasm was nowhere more intense than in Britain where it grew until
botany could be described as a popular recreation. Floricultural journals
abounded, plant-hunters brought in hosts of new wonders, and flower
painting was regarded as a social grace.

Scientific monographs of the period were often opulent – James Bateman's *Orchidaceae of Mexico and Guatemala* (1837-41) was said to be the
largest book ever produced with lithographic plates. The artists for this
work were the otherwise little-known Mrs Withers (fl. 1827-64) and Miss
Drake (fl. 1818-47) 'of Turnham Green'. The lithography was done by a
master noted simply as Gauci, and the anonymous hands that added the
colouring were also highly skilled.

Shortly after the death of Franz Bauer, Kew again became the setting
for an extraordinary figure in the annals of botanical illustration. Whereas

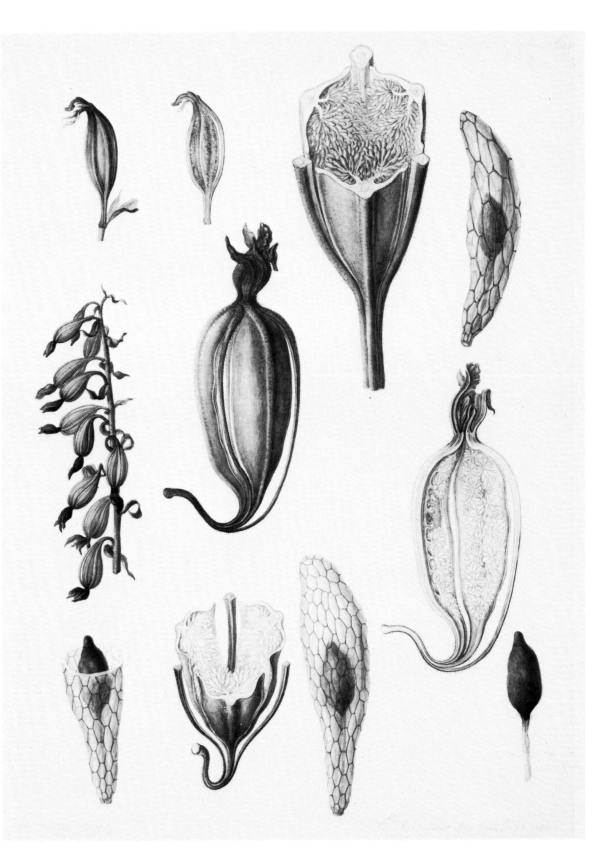

Bauer's work was exceptional in quality, the output of Walter Hood Fitch (1817–92) was all but incredible in quantity. No less than 9960 drawings by him are recorded as having been published; taken as an average of four plates weekly over a span of fifty years, this figure indicates not only his industry but also the awesome fluency that he must have developed.

Fitch, together with his nephew, John Nugent Fitch, stood almost alone in England in maintaining a high standard of lithography. While the skilled use of this medium tended to decline, together with engraving on metal, interest in wood engraving had gradually grown under the stimulus

7 Walter Hood Fitch
(1817–92) *Selenicereus hamatus* (Scheidweiler)
Britton & Rose

16

Osmunda maderiensis

imparted by Thomas Bewick earlier in the century. This growth continued in all areas of illustration until at the close of the nineteenth century wood engraving dominated. At first the process was used for simple, cheap text figures, but greater and greater virtuosity was developed until, with the arrival of photography, engravers were able to simulate its tonal range. Sometimes botanical artists engraved their own works but more often a specialist was used to reproduce every delicate nuance upon the wood-block. Sadly, the craft was swept away when photomechanical methods of reproduction flooded in during the first decades of this century.

Initially this technical advance could scarcely be called a step forward for the botanical artist – drawings reproduced by the new process had to approach the boldness of the early woodcuts to be assured of success. However, developments in printing techniques were rapid, and today it is

8 Sydney Parkinson (1745–71) *Pteris serrulata* drawn in Madeira on Captain Cook's first voyage (1768–71)

17

9 Mary Grierson (1912–)
Crocus baytopiorum Mathew.
In *Curtis's Botanical
Magazine* 1974 Vol.
CLXXX Part 1 N.S. t. 664

possible for a good printer to reproduce the artist's work in colour or in black and white almost in facsimile.

Only a scattering from the names of those who have contributed to the great legacy of botanical art can be included here; a complete record would be a lifetime's study. Current interest has led to the publication of the works of several botanical artists of the past – these include Franz Bauer and, oddly, Marianne North (1830-90) of whom Wilfrid Blunt tartly writes, 'Botanists consider her primarily as an artist; but artists will hardly agree, for her painting is almost wholly lacking in sensibility.' This criticism cannot be applied to the accomplished water-colours of Sydney Parkinson (*c*. 1745-71) which will be seen in a volume shortly to be produced from the archives of the British Museum (Natural History). The bright promise of this young man ended on the 1768 world voyage of Cook, Banks and Solander.

Botanical artists of today include some who are no less gifted than the best of the past: Stella Ross-Craig, Mary Grierson and Margaret Stones in England; Anne Ophelia Dowden, Priscilla Fawcett and Lee Adams in the

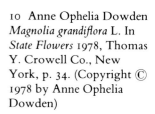

10 Anne Ophelia Dowden *Magnolia grandiflora* L. In *State Flowers* 1978, Thomas Y. Crowell Co., New York, p. 34. (Copyright © 1978 by Anne Ophelia Dowden)

United States; Claus Caspari and Martin Zahn of West Germany; Carlos Riefel in Austria – the list could be extended almost indefinitely from all countries fostering botanical study. Those who wish to know more about botanical artists around the world should purchase the catalogue of the most recent International Exhibition of Botanical Art and Illustration from the Hunt Institute of Botanical Documentation, Carnegie-Mellon University, Pittsburgh, Pennsylvania, USA. Each artist featured is introduced by a potted biography and one or two reduced reproductions of work in the exhibition. This publication indicates that botanical artists flourish through a variety of outlets: positions in Botanical Gardens, Universities and other institutions; freelancing and gallery exhibits; and more than a few both illustrating and writing their own work.

In this bare outline of the evolution of botanical illustration there are inevitably gaps – for instance, the influence of Dutch flower-pieces; or botanical art in the East where realistic flower painting emerged as an independent art form in China in the seventh and eighth centuries AD when, in the West, artists were still slavishly copying debased remains passed down from classical herbalists. For a detailed, erudite, and entirely fascinating account of the history of plant illustration from remote beginnings to the 1950s, I recommend *The Art of Botanical Illustration* by Wilfrid Blunt. This book has been a constant companion for over twenty years, and I am in Mr Blunt's debt not only for the pleasure that his researches have given over such a long period, but also for much of the information in this chapter.

It is hard to imagine what future trends in the field might be, though as the development of botanical illustration has been closely linked to printing, its future may be tied in some degree to information technology. For all that, if a worker of classical times were to be transported to a seat at my drawing table, he would without doubt be able to take up where I left off. He would have no difficulty in recognizing brushes and pigments, though he might marvel at the extended range of the latter. Acrylics might puzzle him, but I am sure that he would quickly feel at home with water-colours and would delight in the quality of the illustration board under his hand. It would not be hard to find him a plant that he would know. Could you or I expect to cope similarly if placed at a botanical artist's desk two thousand years ahead? Will there still be botanical artists? desks? paints? . . . plants?

2 Basic equipment

Equipment and materials used with each medium are discussed in the relevant chapters. However, certain basics are needed no matter what you choose to work in.

WORK SPACE A separate room is desirable; failing that, a space giving some privacy and freedom from interruption, and large enough to allow free movement back from the work in progress to see it as a complete unit. This is especially helpful with larger pieces – in concentrating at close range it is easy to sacrifice the overall effect for the detail. Although in botanical illustration detail is often of prime importance, aesthetic standards and scientific accuracy are rarely at odds, and by viewing occasionally from a distance it is usually possible to meet both requirements. If surroundings are cramped, the effective viewing distance can be doubled by using a mirror. This has the bonus of reversing the image so that the design can be seen in a new way and weaknesses are often shown up. A reducing lens may also be used to see the work as a whole.

LIGHTING The workroom or studio should have good natural lighting, but without bright sunlight. At the least direct sun should be kept from the immediate working area, even if this means putting up a screen of some kind through part of the day. Also, the plant being portrayed should not be backed by a sunlit wall as this will distort tonal structure.

If you are lucky enough to have daylight from windows overhead, together with light from a window at the side to provide modelling for the subject, then you will probably need artificial light only in the early morning and evening. If not, then aim for a good bright system as close to daylight as feasible. Fluorescent lighting overhead coupled with an Anglepoise-type lamp for side-lighting provides an excellent combination. Side-lighting should be from the left if you are right-handed, and vice-versa.

Whatever arrangement is used, there are two essentials: the illumination of the work area must be bright enough for you to see the finest details without strain, and you should be fully aware of colour distortion stemming from the light source. Standard electric lighting is biased towards the yellow to red end of the spectrum, so the effect of yellow or red blooms will be enhanced under artificial light and diminished in daylight. A blue that sparkles in daylight becomes as lead under the lamp, while a poisonous green becomes a pleasing moss hue. The closer daylight is approached, the fewer colour problems will be encountered. It is true that your paintings are going to be seen in artificial light anyway, but tomorrow artificial light may rival the sun.

WORKING SURFACE The working surface can be as primitive as a piece of coreboard (fiberboard) or a similar flat plane, inclined against a pile of books or blocks to give a slope, but a smallish adjustable drawing-board on a large office desk with capacious drawers is more comfortable. Plants in pots can stand on the desk top along with paints, water, brushes etc. A steady table serves the same purpose as a desk, but lacks the useful drawers.

A desk-top adjustable stand may be purchased, to support a drawing-board of any inexpensive material such as plywood or coreboard which will not warp or crack but which can be screwed to the stand. A manufactured drawing-board covered with a white veneer is more expensive. The disadvantage of this system is that the stand will not reliably support a board larger than about 60 × 50 cm (24 × 20 in.). If you are likely to need a bigger surface a drawing- or drafting-stand should be used.

The drawing-stand (fig. 11) has two major advantages and several minor disadvantages. It provides a large working surface which may be raised or lowered and inclined through all positions from the horizontal to the vertical. Against this, there are no drawers except in the more elaborate and very expensive models, all paraphernalia must be moved to a table, and the plant you are working from also has to be put on a separate stand. For large-scale paintings these small irritations must be accepted as it is vital to be able to adjust the board towards the vertical in order to reach the upper portion without discomfort.

Ideally, I would recommend both an adjustable drawing-board and a drawing-stand, the former for most projects, the latter for large-scale work.

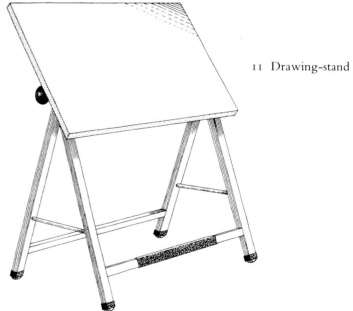

11 Drawing-stand

SEAT Choose a seat which is steady, at the correct height, and comfortable. A drawing-stand is usually, even at its lowest setting, too high for a standard chair, so the alternatives are to stand, to place the chair on a box, or to use a tall stool or a swivel chair (but this can be unsteady). The perfect work seat is one that you are not conscious of using.

PLANT-STAND In portraying plants of all different shapes and sizes, the problem is to position each one at eye-level (unless a high or low viewpoint is needed for a specific reason). I have used many sorts of clamps and stands but no single one has suited every situation. A handyman might consider making a multi-purpose stand similar to the one sketched in fig. 12.

12 Design for a plant-stand

HAND-LENS This is indispensable. It should magnify by about eight to ten diameters. Though details seen through the lens may not appear in completed drawings, it is essential to understand how plant parts fit together to avoid suggesting ambiguities. And, as a bonus, unexpected wonders and beauties are revealed. A novice often holds the lens close to the object with the eye at some distance; this gives a tiny field of view and is much less satisfactory than putting the lens to the eye and raising the object until it is in sharp focus.

DISSECTING MICROSCOPE Work requiring the use of a microscope is usually done at a scientific institution; but if you can afford a microscope for work at home be sure, first, that you purchase an instrument suitable for working on topics such as seeds or flower dissections. A capacity of × 20 to × 80 or × 100 is sufficient; higher magnification than this moves into the specialized field of cell-structure which is outside the scope of this book. Even at 100 diameters the depth of field becomes wafer-thin and a lesser enlargement is usually more useful. Secondly, a choice has to be made between an instrument with a zoom-lens and the turret type in which different lenses are moved into position for each of the several set magnifications. If the *stated* magnification is the same as the *actual* magnification (and it rarely is), the turret type might be preferred; by a small movement of the hand you can select the desired setting, read off the micrometer eyepiece scale (an essential accessory) and multiply for transfer to the drawing. But if the stated magnification is inaccurate by even a small amount, a complex conversion has to be made for every measurement taken. The advantage of a zoom-lensed model is that a mark can be made on the instrument where the required settings actually occur.

CAMERA In some situations it is necessary to turn to the camera as an aid. You may want to portray rare plants that it would be criminal to pick, and though fairly simple line drawings may be carried out *in situ*, a detailed study is often impracticable. Or lack of time may prevent individual plates from being completed – though to some extent this problem can be eased by keeping plants in the refrigerator or by potting them up for later use.

The point to be stressed is that photographs should be used only where there is no other sensible means of access to the necessary information. And never – or almost never – use photographs taken by anyone else unless they are taken in your company or you have an intimate knowledge of the species concerned. I can recollect only four occasions in over twenty years when I have had to use a photograph taken by another's hand. In each instance the fact that the illustration was based on a photograph was noted in a caption, as I felt slightly uneasy that something might have been

missed that would have been clear had I been able to see the living flowers.
For hints on photographing plants and choice of camera, see chapter 11.

DIVIDERS Used to take dimensions directly from the model; and by 'walking' the points across the paper, magnifications of up to × 5 or so may be rapidly recorded. Dividers are faster to manoeuvre through foliage than a ruler.

PROPORTIONAL DIVIDERS Many botanical illustrators favour this instrument. By a pre-selected setting, a dimension described by the distance between the points of the two larger arms is reflected in a correct reduction between the points of the two smaller arms (a reversal of the dividers will provide magnification when needed). You may want to reduce a plant or its parts by, say, half: move the setting device to the appropriate reading and separate the major points until they match the dimension to be taken; the minor points will then be at half scale and can be applied to the paper. To avoid leaving ugly scratches or holes in the work, the tool should be placed flush or parallel with the surface, with the long blades facing away for safety; a slight pressure towards the tips will then record the dimension on the paper as two small dots – alternatively, pencil marks may be used.

POCKET CALCULATOR This is invaluable, especially when drawing flower dissections or converting measurements from a photograph.

PRICKER A needle-like steel rod set in a holder, useful for transferring traced drawings with precision (see p. 94). The instrument may be purchased, or you can use a dissecting-needle or other sharp point.

SCALPEL AND DISSECTING NEEDLES A scalpel is the only sensible cutting tool to use for flower dissections.
Dissecting needles hold the plant part firmly in place while the scalpel is being used. I like to use two forms, one bent at an angle to its holder and the other straight. The angled kind is perfect for holding tissues in place without actually piercing them, and the straight one may be used for delicate probing.
Scalpel blades and dissecting needles should not contact the stage of the microscope as they will mar the surface. All operations should be carried out over glass such as microscope slides or petri dishes.

CRAFT KNIFE A heavy-duty craft knife (mat knife) will serve for pencil sharpening, cutting paper and illustration board etc. The kind with a retractable blade is safer than the fixed variety.

FEATHER A feather is ideal for brushing away eraser particles.

INVISIBLE MENDING TAPE Excellent for holding paper firmly in place on the drawing-board; it may be pulled away after use without lifting the fibres of the paper surface or tearing its edges. Masking tape and sellotape (Scotch tape) are far less satisfactory. An eraser will remove sticky traces left by tape.

3 Concepts

Perspective

This topic is too lengthy to cover here, and I would refer you to any good general art book. However, you need only master the essential principles: botanical illustration rarely requires anything more involved, but shaky perspective can ruin an otherwise convincing plate.

Colour-mixing

Most readers will already have some understanding of colour-mixing. The main problem will be in mixing colours to match precisely what you see in the plant. For instance, you may know that blue mixed with yellow yields green, but this is only the first step in trying to match the hue of a particular leaf. A touch of red or a hint of crimson may be needed, and perhaps a little of another blue or a different yellow. An analysis has to be made of each colour to be matched. This skill develops through experience, and before long you should be able to carry out a colour breakdown unconsciously as you are mixing. Specific suggestions are given in chapters 9 and 10.

Tone-values

Except for work done in pure outline, insufficient attention to tone-values often spoils a painting or drawing of a plant. The tone-value of a colour refers to its quality of 'lightness' or 'darkness'. If a plant is photographed in black and white, the resulting print will represent colours by a range from white to black. If the same plant is then photographed in colour it will be seen that each colour on the photograph is recorded on the black and white print as a patch of 'tone' in 'value' anywhere from white, through all the greys, to black. Fig. 13 illustrates the range of tone-values broken into ten steps. Take a piece of leaf or any pigmented material and move it along the diagram until the 'lightness' or 'darkness' is matched, and there you will have its tone-value.

13 Tone-values

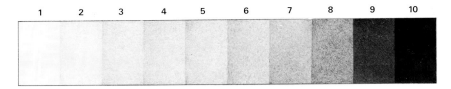

Botanical knowledge

Your effectiveness as a botanical artist, and your pleasure in your work, will be enhanced by building a background of plant-lore. There are excellent 'outline' books available such as Peter Raven's *Biology of Plants* or J. M. Lowson's *Textbook of Botany* (see Bibliography).

It is satisfying to know every species of a genus, to be aware of the characters by which one species may be distinguished from another, to look for a representative of 'your' genus in suitable habitats, and to compare details of minute form and structure.

As well as having common names, plants also have Latin names based on the binomial system invented by Linnaeus and developed since. Here I wish only to point out the advantage of using scientific names in gaining an understanding of relationships. The use of 'common' or 'vernacular' names alone can easily be misleading. For example, *Erythronium americanum* is also known as trout-lily and as dog-tooth violet, yet it is neither trout-like nor a violet, though it is a lily. Common names also vary according to locality, whereas scientific names are stable (excepting when new studies change the interpretation of relationships, as in the recent merging of the genus *Zauschneria* into the genus *Epilobium*).

Self-criticism

Each painting, each drawing, each illustration should be better than the last. Measure yourself against your own work and that of others. When starting on a project, try to find something similar by another artist, see how he has solved like problems, and then strive to go one better. This examination of the attempts of fellow artists is very worth while - one can learn from, and share their pleasure.

Accuracy

In working for taxonomic purposes, each plant portrayed is not only an individual, distinct and apart, it must also be seen as a representative of a particular *taxon* (form, variety, subspecies, species etc.). In other words it represents a group. It is necessary to be sure that the individual portrayed has all the characteristics associated with the group. These are easily checked in detail if there are published descriptions to compare with the specimen, or, if the illustration is for a new monograph or revision, the author may like you to use his manuscript. Though the author may have a number of the plants that you are illustrating growing in the experimental garden, or available from the wild, there is no guarantee that every one of them will conform to the description for the group. You and your work, not the plant, are more likely to be blamed for deviation from the printed word. Let me give an example. I had drawn a dissection of the *corolla* of a small heath showing internal hairs. A botanist, looking at the species afresh after some years, examined my drawing and commented that the corolla should not show hairs on the inside surface. There was no convincing answer to this other than to find the plant long forgotten and to demonstrate the veracity of the study. The same heath was found in the experimental garden carrying the same identification as the drawing - even though the tag had almost faded away after ten years or so. Flowers were present and so were the disputed hairs.

4 Plant handling

Plant portraits may give problems of two main kinds apart from those caused by deficiencies in the artist: some arise from the medium or the style chosen; others are inherent in the plants themselves.

Phenotypic variation

One source of difficulty is *phenotypic* variation. All living organisms may be thought of in terms of their *genotype* or genetic structure, and their *phenotype* or appearance due to the response of the genotype to external factors. Two plants of the same genotype grown in the same conditions will look much alike; but grown under entirely different regimes, their phenotypic responses may be such as to make them appear to be separate species. This is an oversimplification; the interested reader will find that these terms represent the tip of a very large iceberg.

Problems may arise when, for example, a plant which normally grows at a high altitude is gathered and grown on for a period. It will often develop characteristics quite other than those shown on its rocky peak. There, in response to higher levels of solar radiation, its leaves would have a reddish or coppery pigmentation, and harsh conditions might impose a compact form. At a lower elevation, the leaf pigmentation would probably revert to green, and the form of the plant might become tall, lush and open. This kind of change is not unusual – though some species will vary little through a broad spectrum of growing conditions. You may be embarrassed in faithfully recording the plant in hand if you know little of the same plants in the bush. To avoid distortion from phenotypic plasticity, the best approach is to use authentic fresh material from the subject's typical habitat.

Growth-phase

Distortion can also occur when plants either have not reached maturity or are in decline. In both phases flower size may be affected – the first and last flowers are often smaller than those of the plant in full prime. Again, in the *ontogeny* (life-history) of an individual, juvenile leaves – often less toothed or dissected – may be very much in evidence before maturition, remaining or partly present at maturity, absent or decaying in senescence.

Models

Subject to the reservations mentioned above, the ideal plant model is one growing healthily in a pot. With some species it is possible (depending upon their conservation status - see pp. 11, 31) to take a plant from the wild complete with roots and soil, pot it up, allow it to stabilize (twenty-four hours in a water bath sometimes helps, plus a couple of days in the shade) portray it, and then make it into a voucher herbarium specimen (p. 30). Other plants wilt when lifted and these have to be drawn immediately if this is feasible, or must be grown from seed. If neither course is practicable it may be necessary to use photography allied with dried specimens, field notes etc. Naturally the dimensions of the plant also have some bearing upon treatment.

Sometimes a plant which collapses after potting will revive for long enough to be drawn if it is placed in a container of water after washing out the roots.

A flowering branch, or a single flower or other detail, can be placed in a jar of water. For the tiny portion, a small shallow receptacle – a petri dish or similar – with cotton-wool or blotting paper soaked in water, will create a micro-climate of moist air, essential when working with delicate membraneous tissues in a warm dry atmosphere. The upper section of a petri dish can be placed over the lower to increase the greenhouse effect if you have to leave the work for some minutes. If the plant material is light in tone, stain the cotton-wool or blotting paper with ink or paint to obtain enough contrast between the subject and the background. This is also useful when examining plant parts carrying hairs which may not be visible against a light ground.

Dissections

Often the technique of flower dissection is clothed by a certain amount of humbug. A dissecting needle or two, a sharp scalpel, a good eye and a steady hand are all that are generally required. For minute organs the dissecting microscope will also be used. Small objects are more easily handled if they are embedded lightly in a low-temperature wax or other malleable substance. Scalpel blades lose their edge quickly: rather than replacing them after little use, I prefer to maintain sharpness by frequent use of a fine-grained stone. Resistant tissue is sometimes more amenable if a moistened blade is used. A dissecting needle is used to hold the object still while cutting. Speed is important as tissues rapidly deteriorate during dissection – with flowers, for example, though all measurements should be taken from one specimen, it is worth while to have others available to provide supplementary information. Details of a typical dissection are given in chapter 7.

Sometimes a botanist will need to make a dissection in order to point out special features, but it is usually better to use this only as a guide. In my experience, the illustrator will make an improved dissection to draw from, having perhaps a clearer understanding of the requirements for illustration. It is a pleasurable experience to remove an organ, a pistil perhaps less than a millimetre tall, cleanly and without damage and to place it in a position for drawing; but the dissection of small flowers etc. calls for the greatest patience as well as dexterity. So often, within reach of success, required material will be damaged by an inadvertent movement.

Lighting and placement

Plant illustrations are in the main shaded on the right-hand side, suggesting light falling from the upper left which, for the right-handed artist, will not throw a shadow from the working hand on to the drawing. The reverse is true for the left-hander who will find it more convenient to have the light source on the right. With individual plates it does not matter which side the light appears to be from, but for a set of illustrations it is better if the lighting is consistent. The same is true for plant details surrounding a habit study (fig. 65).

The plant model should stand in correct relation to your eye; normally the portion being worked on should be kept at about eye-level. This means that with a tall specimen, starting with the *inflorescence*, it may be necessary to raise the plant two or more times, giving a view of separate sections on the illustration. One point worth emphasis is that the specimen should be viewed from exactly the same point while each section is being drawn: as the model will be close – ideally, 30–60 cm (12–24 in.) from the eye – even small movements of the head will change what can or cannot be seen and will render a complex structure almost impossible to manage. For the same reason it is best to favour one eye in viewing; the other should briefly be closed or covered. With especially difficult topics, choose a specific point on the plant which may be aligned with a mark on the background. Make sure from time to time that the original viewpoint is being held, by checking that the spot on the plant and the mark behind are superimposed. The background mark must be made by someone else, while you sit comfortably in the exact working position and select the two points by eye.

With a simple subject the foregoing tactic is not needed. However, for both simple and complex items you should not be over-hasty in starting to draw. Once the specimen is at eye-level, turn it around slowly a couple of times before selecting the best aspect. If the plant has just been brought indoors it may also be advisable to allow it time to adjust to new light conditions. With a rigid species such as a cactus or a succulent no period of adjustment is needed, but with non-woody flexible models it is surprising how much twisting and turning occurs. In some species virtually all parts move to present themselves to the brightest source of light. This is another reason for blocking direct sun from the studio – it is more than annoying when a light-sensitive plant swings away from an artificial light to track a moving band of sunshine.

A plant should be allowed an hour or so for settling in the studio since, as well as moving towards the light, flowers sometimes react strongly to a new regime – commonly petals flex open more widely, buds burst, and anthers *dehisce* (open to expose pollen).

Storage

Frequently plants are held over from one day to another. If your model is growing in a pot it may be left with safety overnight, but if, for instance, another growth phase is required which may occur some days later, it is usually best to return the plant to its usual situation to avoid distortion from growth indoors. When fragments or cut stems are held they often freshen if they are placed, still in their container, overnight inside a plastic bag: this should be of stiffish quality to ensure that it will stand free of its contents – petals and other delicate parts may otherwise cling to condensation on the inner surface. Many specimens also benefit (bagged or not) from a stay in the refrigerator – the chill moist air has a rejuvenating effect.

If you have more cut plants than can be managed for several days, decay may be inhibited by placing them in the refrigerator. Some species will stay in excellent condition for a long time in this way – alpine plant cuttings have stayed in prime condition for approaching six months. Flowers usually deteriorate before foliage, so they should be given priority for drawing. Note that chilling, not freezing, is the aim – the tissues of frozen plants break down quickly upon thawing.

For realistic plant portraits without specific scientific intent, pressing and drying (see below) will also preserve material for later access. The professional botanical illustrator, however, will inevitably need to use to a greater or lesser extent the organized facilities of an herbarium.

Herbarium specimens

Herbaria are collections of dried and pressed plants, filed alphabetically or according to an accepted system of classification, for reference and study. They range in size from the small, perhaps home-based, special-purpose assemblage to the herbarium of a great scientific institution holding millions of specimens from all parts of the world. Botanical illustrators employed by scientific establishments may spend a large proportion of their time working directly from herbarium specimens. And, when live plants are illustrated, these also are generally processed into 'voucher' specimens as a matter of routine. In either case an illustration will be associated with a preserved plant, and a caption should record the plant's sheet identification – a number prefixed by the international code letters assigned to the herbarium.

The value of a plate is enormously enhanced when it is cross-referenced to a particular herbarium sheet: the specimen may serve to confirm the veracity of the drawing, and botanical workers are enabled to examine both the illustration and the specimen as required throughout the several hundred years that they may be extant. If the illustration was made solely from a dried specimen, it can show only those characteristics retained after processing; yet many details may be illuminated that otherwise could be deciphered only by intensive study. And if the illustration was made from a living plant, it may convey information no longer present or obscured in the dried specimen – features such as natural posture of leaves and flowers, secreting hairs, glossiness, succulence and so on.

Professional botanical artists will not normally be called upon to prepare herbarium specimens, but there may be occasions when it may be helpful to preserve a plant for later examination. Detailed instructions on the many methods used for drying can be found in books dealing with botanical collecting. All the methods have in common the objective of drying the specimens as quickly as possible without the use of more than a very gentle heat. Excessive heat causes severe discoloration and results, at best, in very inferior specimens.

The simplest method consists of pressing the plant material between sheets of absorbent paper – old newspaper will do nicely – and then changing the papers every day until the specimens are quite dry. Pressure can be provided by any convenient heavy object, such as old books or, if the papers are sandwiched between boards, by straps.

The artist will appreciate more than most people the qualities needed in a good botanical specimen. Ideally, the specimen should illustrate all the features of the species. This may be easy with small species as the whole plant, or even a sample of the population, can conveniently be pressed. But with large herbs, not to mention trees and shrubs, only a small part of the whole plant can be preserved. The missing information can, to some extent, be provided by careful notes, e.g. height, branching pattern, bark colour and texture; and, for all specimens, notes on flower colour and scent and any other features that are difficult to preserve, should be made. Photographs, carefully coordinated with dried specimens, can be of particular value to illustrate the general appearance of plants that are too large to preserve as normal specimens.

Before collecting any specimens in the wild, you should be familiar with local legislation governing conservation, and in any case you should never collect specimens unless the species concerned is plentiful in that particular area.

Herbarium specimens are intended for use, and the scientific illustrator should consult additional sheets as background, whether working from living or dried specimens. Each herbarium has its own rules and these should be carefully observed: their main intent will be to ensure that each specimen is preserved for as long as possible consonant with its function as a botanical tool.

Lichens, mosses and liverworts (usually housed in packets in the herbarium), ferns, grasses, many conifers, and other groups, are often little altered as dried specimens from their appearance in life. Apart from slight difficulties which may be found in translating pressed parts into realistic perspective, such plants should not test the illustrator more than they would have done in life. But species with delicate, easily damaged tissues may well give problems – flowers for example are vulnerable to distortion during drying and pressing. Sometimes flowers from the same collection will have been preserved in spirits, and then it is usually straightforward to use a substitute in drawing, as these blooms will appear in structure much as they did in life. If this solution is not available, dessicated tissues of crushed flowers etc. may be partially re-inflated by detaching them from the sheet (where this is permissible) and immersing them in boiling water for a minute or two. After use the fragments should be restored to the sheet in one of the small envelopes or packets used by the herbarium.

Though drawing from herbarium specimens has disadvantages, there are some gains. A major one is that the model is fixed in time at whatever point in its cycle it was collected: it can be put aside and picked up again unchanged years later if necessary, while with live plants a number of needed species may flower at around the same time. Also, the actual handling of herbarium specimens in comparison with live models is usually easier. The sheet can be conveniently placed on the working surface and may easily be manoeuvred under the dissecting microscope.

As a rule, some direction will be given as to which features on the sheet are of special botanical interest, and the artist will ensure that these are clearly shown. Beyond this it will often be useful to introduce an element of tonal emphasis, particularly when the material to be drawn is poorly differentiated. Emphasizing some parts in greater detail and darker tone than their surrounds will give the drawing a slightly three-dimensional quality and make the work easier to 'read'. Sharp photographs or colour slides may be used as aids, but do not rely on reportage or on others' illustrations.

Since many features are modified in drying and pressing, a restrained illustrative treatment is best, relying mainly on line, with tone kept to a minimum. Ink is the ideal medium for this purpose (chapter 7).

Experienced botanical illustrators are able to reconstruct the appearance of a living plant from a herbarium specimen by calling on their background knowledge and 'feel' for their subjects – even though often they will not have seen the plant in its live form. This accumulated experience is different from that of the scientist but complementary; and when the two are brought together, the best possible results are seen.

5 Plants in detail

This chapter contains observations about various kinds of plants, plant parts, and their characteristics. Apart from the first model, it is biased towards flowering plants as they are more familiar to most readers and the nomenclature of their parts is less esoteric than for some groups. Nevertheless, the structures detailed have their counterparts elsewhere, and information given here may be used in drawing like forms wherever they occur.

The plants in fig. 14 demonstrate the variety of combinations that exist. Here we will look at some of the items helpful to the artist confronted by this diversity and at the basic steps of transferring data about the plants to paper – before tone, ink or water-colour etc. are used.

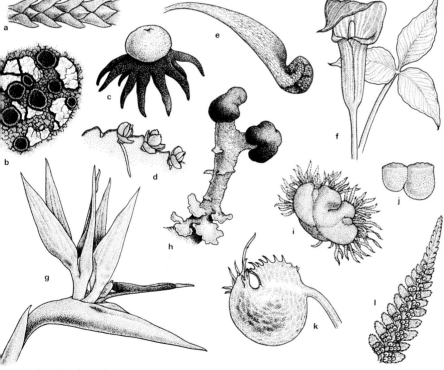

14 A selection of diverse plant structures: **a** *Libocedrus bidwillii*, a detail of closely appressed conifer leaves; **b** *Rhizocarpon geographicum*, crustose lichen (enlarged); **c** *Astraeus hygrometricus*, earth star fungus; **d** *Kalenchoë daigremontiana*, the maternity plant – margin of leaf with plantlets; **e** *Sarracenia psittacina*, pitcher plant – prostrate pitcher; **f** *Arisaema triphyllum*, Jack in the pulpit; **g** *Strelitzia reginae*, bird of paradise plant – inflorescence; **h** *Cladonia* sp., magnified portion of lichen; **i** *Ricciocarpus natans*, a water-dwelling liverwort; **j** *Wolffia arrhiza* var. *australiana*, of the duckweed family (enlarged); **k** *Utricularia novae-zelandiae*, bladder wort – magnified bladder trap; **l** *Dryopteris felis-mas*, male fern – frond underside

A basic sketch

Several general principles emerge in drawing a fungus species – one of the simplest forms (fig. 15).

The model was placed at eye-level, examined from all sides, and the most pleasing aspect chosen. Initially I intended to draw only one specimen, but as the underside *gills* must also be seen, I included another, tilted to expose the required detail.

SIZE AND SCALE Pencil and paper were selected with the finishing medium in mind and need not be discussed here except for one point – paper size. A common error is to cut a sheet so that the subject extends to the edges. This may create problems of handling, especially if the work is to be printed. Plan your plate layout first. For this exercise it was assumed that the plants were to be drawn life-scale. I took the outside dimensions with dividers, taking care that measurements were made on one plane (see below); these were used to work out an arrangement leaving ample margins. Sometimes it is not easy to reach a prior determination of size, or you may be unsure of just how much of the subject is needed on paper until it is sketched in. In these cases, work on an over-sized sheet until dimensions are settled.

If plates are to form a set, all of the same scale on the same sized sheets, you may have to juggle to fit the subject on the paper within fixed dimensions. When working on a series of such plates, perhaps portraying a genus, you may find that, with the exception of one or two species, all fit life-size within the framework. The over-sized species may be drawn life-size, showing less of their habit than those of the other plates; or be reduced in scale and still remain within the existing frame; or be drawn still at life-size, and showing the same proportion of the subjects as the rest of the series, yet within a larger framework on a larger sheet. Either of the first two choices should be made if there is no measurable loss of botanical worth. Occasionally the last possibility has to be chosen; then, if there is an appreciable difference in size from the other plates, the increased reduction on publication is usually visible – no matter what care is taken in adjusting line-thicknesses, detail etc. – so breaking the consistent appearance of the set.

I decided that the margins for the fungus plate should be 3 cm (*c.* $1\frac{1}{4}$ in.) at the top and sides and 3.5 cm ($1\frac{3}{8}$ in.) at the bottom (nearly all art works appear optically centred if a slightly wider space is left at the lower edge). These margin sizes will serve for the smallest plate up to an image height of around 30 cm (12 in.); you will see when wider ones are needed.

STARTING TO DRAW At this stage I had a sheet of appropriate size with margins, marked in very lightly, based on the outside dimensions of the fungi. The next step was to decide where to start drawing. I usually lightly block-in the whole drawing to establish that it is going to work as planned, and then move to and fro, strengthening and correcting until completion. The procedure for blocking-in is to take the major element of the composition – in this instance the fungus on the left – and to build around it. An appraisal of the form (see also p. 36) was made, and salient points were selected for measurement; these are shown on fig. 15 as small crosses connected by broken lines (in an actual drawing the broken lines would not be put in and the crosses would be made very faintly).

As the drawing was life-sized, dimensions were transferred to the paper by means of dividers, taking care to avoid sloping the dividers away from an imaginary vertical plane passing through the model. For instance, placing the point of one arm at point *A*, the other arm must be held in the same vertical plane and adjusted until it is level with point *B*. If to do this

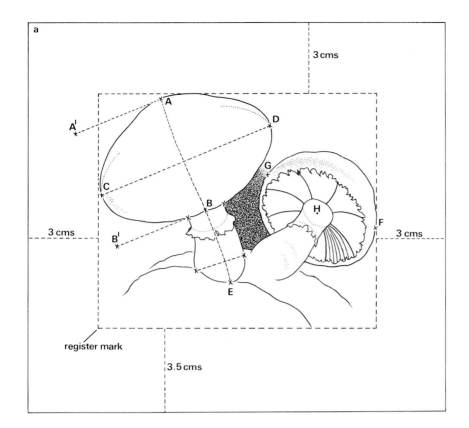

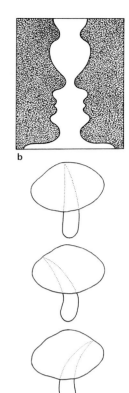

a
3 cms
A
A¹
D
C
G
B
H
F
3 cms
B¹
3 cms
E
register mark
3.5 cms

b

c

the lower arm had been tilted forward until point B was touched, the measure obtained, though life-size, would have been uncorrected for perspective and would introduce a considerable error. In this case it was necessary to move the divider arms out to points A^1 and B^1 to make a measurement free from obstruction.

Unless you are working on a complex topic such as a flower dissection, few measurements are required. For the present subject only the total height, width of the cap, width of the stem where it moved from view under the cap, and the thickness of the stem at the base were used. In practice one tends to sketch in more or less as the measurements are made – there is no rigid sequence.

PERSPECTIVE   After the major component, the left-hand fungus, was drawn, the fungus on the right was put in; and this serves to illustrate a small difficulty. You will notice that the right-hand form is slightly to the rear of the other, i.e. further from the observer; so in order to show it correctly in perspective its actual dimensions were reduced by careful assessment by eye against the measured and drawn-in dimensions of the first fungus.

To avoid distortion one eye was used to view from a fixed position. Next, point F was defined where the curve of the cap intersected the line of the margin on the right. The ellipse passing through F and G was sketched in and particular care was taken in estimating the positions of G and H. Placing the stem and the exposed underside was then easy.

15 **a** basic sketch;
b 'balustrade/profile' effect;
c siting of caps on stems

ANALYSIS OF FORMS AND SPACES For the second fungus another concept was helpful. The pattern of the toadstool forms implied a pattern of space – an appreciation of the interplay of forms is gained by considering the shapes between them. This is illustrated by the well-known illusion in fig. 15*b* – a white balustrade or human profiles? A white form creates two black patterns of space – two black forms create a white space pattern. In fig. 15*a*, stipple indicates one pattern of space; it is abstract, so the eye tends not to be led astray by a subjective appreciation of the way it ought to appear – perspective and foreshortening do not apply.

Though the forms of the fungi are simple, they may provide a number of further pointers. Earlier it was noted that 'an appraisal of the form was made'. This mental analysis becomes automatic with practice. Complex shapes are broken down into their basic components – ellipses, cones, circles, squares etc. – in order that they may be more easily handled. In the present example the components were two dome shapes and two cylinders – not difficult forms provided care is taken with the ellipses.

When placing one unit upon another – domes on cylinders, caps on stems, flowers on stalks – it is easy to create a wrong impression by even a tiny deviation from accuracy around the section where one component joins the other. This is because the eye tends to follow an indicated subjective line. If lines are projected as shown in fig. 15*c* such errors should not occur.

The gills of the right-hand fungus radiate around the point of entry of the stem (H). To show this – and any other types of radiating lines or forms – it is helpful to mark in a hypothetical point from which they originate. Then the positions of several key-lines are drawn (see heavier lines on the sketch) and the rest can be placed with confidence.

Recorded subtle fluctuations in outline are one of the marks of careful observation. At a glance the curve of the cap of the left-hand fungus in fig. 15*a* might appear smooth, but a closer examination shows small but distinct variations in outline. The same kind of detail is seen about the rim of the cap of the second fungus along the outer edge of the gills.

STEP BY STEP SUMMARY The procedure outlined above should be useful for most types of botanical illustration: (*a*) place model carefully, choosing the most pleasing and useful aspect; (*b*) select sheet-size using overall dimensions of subject; (*c*) lightly mark in margins; (*d*) measure off and put in key-points; (*e*) establish background and other material by eye using the measured major components as guides; (*f*) move over drawing, adding detail, strengthening and correcting. The drawing can then be finished in the chosen medium.

We can now move from basic procedure to an examination of some of the more common plant structures and the challenges they present. Botanical terms are used sparingly – it is not intended that each section should provide a guide to nomenclature, or that the complete range of forms should be covered; for these topics botanical texts should be consulted.

Leaves

There are features common to virtually all leaves and the characteristic expression of each feature may be of importance.

OUTLINES As you look at a plant stem you will often see that the leaves at the bottom have a different outline from those at the top, and you should watch for such changes as well as for differences characteristic of the leaves of separate species. Taking a simple outline first, fig. 16a, there are several items of interest even in this uncomplicated shape. The widest measure is slightly oblique, falling from left to right, and the dimension of the widest part of the leaf on the left of the midrib is less than that on the right. The leaf tip attenuates to a fine point and the base of the *lamina* or blade passes smoothly into the *petiole* or stalk. The petiole is one–fifth of the length of the lamina.

16 Leaf forms: **a** simple;
b palmate; **c** dissected;
d pinnate

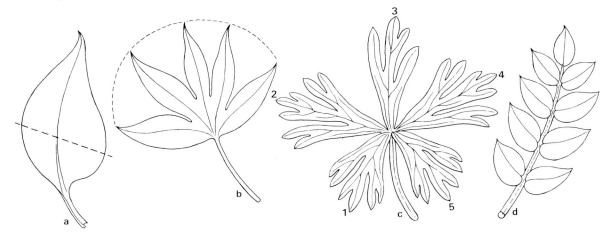

Quite small variations will alter the character of a leaf, changing its appearance and its botanical description. Several likely variations are shown in fig. 17. These emphasize the care that should be taken in drawing, as such differences are sometimes stable enough in separate species to be used as part of the process of identification. Note that the only differences between *a*, *b* and *c* are those imposed by moving the widest portion of the

17 Significant changes in leaf morphology brought about by small variations in outline

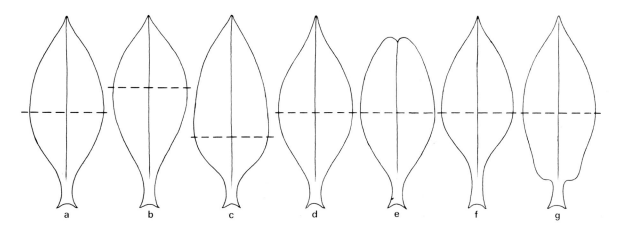

lamina from a line through the mid-section to above and below it. In *d* and *e*, the leaf apices alone are changed – all other characters remain as in *a*. In *f* and *g* only the leaf bases have been altered. By tinkering with three characters – the position of the widest portion of the leaf and the shape of the leaf apex and base – seven quite distinct outlines have been made. In nature, the widths of the leaves and the lengths of the petioles might also be varied (sometimes petioles will be absent and such leaves are termed *sessile*). These and other characters may be shuffled to give a tremendous number of possibilities.

This section started with a discussion of the leaf outline in fig. 16*a*. In the more complex shapes of *b*, *c* and *d*, it is clear that much the same questions should be asked in analysing the basic shapes and noting key dimensions (as in the fungus sketch); taking special care with the leaf bases and apices; noting the length of the petiole; and any other particular characteristics. Two further general points will be treated in more depth later: first, note the form of the base of the petiole where it attaches to the stem or branch; second, the angle at which the leaf joins the stem – its posture – may also be characteristic.

A third component may or may not be present with the lamina and the petiole. This is the *stipule*, which may be found (usually paired) at the petiole base (fig. 18). It ranges from being a leafy appendage as shown here to being hair-like or a minute scale, or absent.

Though *pinnate* leaves such as that shown in fig. 16*d* may look complex, their structure really is quite simple. The more difficult palmate leaf shape at *b* has been reduced to its basic outline; in nature it might appear as shown, or be complicated by various secondary toothing (*serration*) or dissection. In these forms it is often advisable initially to reduce the outline to its basic elements as at *b*; the points of the lobes of this leaf fall helpfully along a curve (this is not uncommon). It may also be useful to measure off the distances between these points, especially when working on leaves such as *c* where one would measure the lengths of the radiating lobes and the distances between the numbered points.

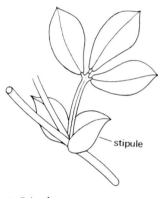

stipule

18 Stipules

LEAF MARGINS After considering basic leaf outlines, look closer at their margins. In essence, leaf margins may be simple or *linear* (without teeth); toothed in a variety of ways; hidden by being turned under or *revolute*; or wavy, *undulate*.

The main task is to discern the pattern and then to represent it accurately. Usually this is straightforward, though some margin types are difficult owing either to complexity of detail or to ambiguities introduced in portraying three dimensions upon a two-dimensional surface. This latter problem is typified by the leaf with an undulate margin (fig. 19*d*). Unless the greatest care is taken it may appear in a drawing that the blade becomes wider and narrower – moving in and out in relation to the midrib, as in *c*, rather than up and down in the vertical plane. Close observation with judicious use of shadows and highlights will avoid this impression.

In illustration, leaf margins display degrees of hairiness rather better than leaf surfaces where hairs may be obscured. Also, the thickness of a leaf may be revealed by touches along the edges.

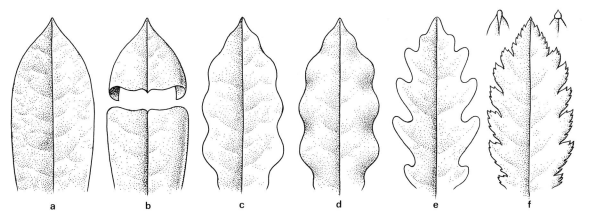

Leaves may show a tiny protruberance, *mucro*, at the tips of the margin teeth, and/or at the leaf apex. These are often different in texture from the rest of the leaf and should be shown where feasible (fig. 19*f*).

VENATION AND SURFACE MODELLING Leaf *venation* is often responsible for the surface patterning of the lamina. This influence is direct when the veins are clearly seen against the body of the leaf due to differences in tone and/or colouring, and indirect when the veins remain indistinct with their positions revealed by rucking and modelling. Often the conditions are present together – distinct venation and a sculpted surface as in fig. 20*c*.

Patterns of venation are distinctive in many groups. Parallel venation (fig. 20*e*), for example, is seen in most *monocotyledonous* plants, though even within this fundamental design there is room for variety; *dicotyledonous* taxa show a great variety of veining. Note whether veins oppose or alternate with each other along the midrib, or whether they originate at the leaf base. The ways in which the veins terminate are also important – sometimes they will follow through to a tooth tip, or they may join another major vein just inside the leaf margin and then swing away to the apex. Major veins should be accurate as to numbers and arrangement. Sometimes the minor veins are seen just as distinctly, forming a complicated reticulation. You may be sufficiently skilful to show the whole network on each leaf, but if this were done, one species might absorb the time assigned to many. Also, curiously, if an attempt is made to put in each tiny vein to scale and with no extra emphasis, the overall effect is more often than not unconvincing – a generalized impression usually appears more realistic. Avoid over-emphasizing main veins and midribs if they are obscure in life: an exception might be made for work done from

19 Leaf margins: **a** entire; **b** revolute; **c** sinuate; **d** undulate; **e** lobed; **f** serrate – in this instance, as the larger divisions carry secondary toothing, the condition is more precisely described as 'double-serrate'

20 Venation and surface modelling: **a** surface smooth, veins obscure; **b** surface smooth, veins distinct; **c** surface modelled, veins distinct; **d** surface modelled, veins obscure; **e** parallel venation

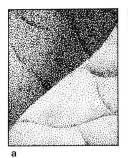

herbarium specimens. Although drying often obliterates surface modelling, it sometimes exposes venation, which may be illustrated since a somewhat diagrammatic version of the plant is inevitable when using dried material.

LEAVES IN PERSPECTIVE Walter Hood Fitch expressed good sense on this subject in 1869 in an article in *The Gardeners' Chronicle:* 'Leaves have been subjected to more bad treatment by the draughtsman than perhaps any other portion of the vegetable kingdom; they have been represented, or rather misrepresented, in all kinds of impossible positions. Numerous are the tortures to which they have been subjected: dislocated or broken ribs, curious twists, painful to behold – even wretched veins have not escaped; and all these errors in perspective arise from inattention to the simple fact, that in a curved leaf, showing the underside, the midrib should be continuous, and the veins should spring from the midrib.'

Drawing leaves in perspective in all their varied postures is largely a matter of observation. As Fitch implies, the midrib is the prime structure; once this is established the rest is less testing. Complex toothing or serrations are more challenging when leaves are twisted or viewed from the side or below – it is helpful to sketch the margins in very lightly, after placing the midrib, and then to use the main veins as guides to position teeth, serrations or lobes. Fig. 21 shows several common situations.

21 Leaves in perspective:
a-d steps in progression;
e some common forms in perspective

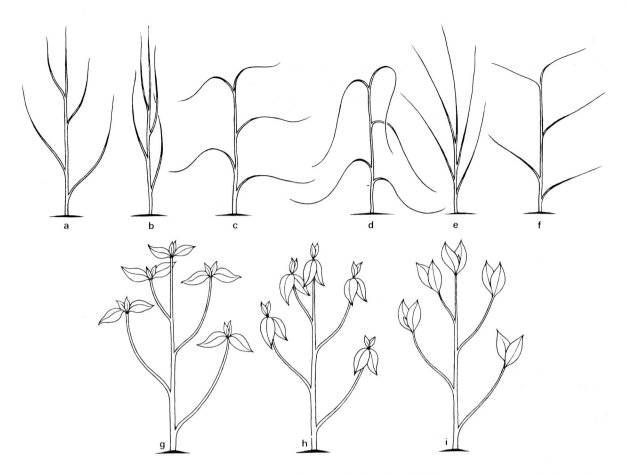

POSTURES OF LEAVES, BRANCHES AND STEMS Posture is related to *habit*, that is, the general appearance of the plant due to the particular way in which the stem or stems emerge from the ground, the mode of branching (if any), the way the leaves sit, and the type of inflorescence etc.

Posture is vital in capturing the character of a species. It may be analysed in terms of angles. The angles which stems and branches maintain in relation to each other and to the ground may be constant. This is less true of many leaves since their posture is more likely to change according to their stage of development, water stress, whether it is day or night, position in relation to the sun, etc. The above points are demonstrated in fig. 22. A simple hypothetical plant form is shown and its four bare branches are moved through several plausible postures (*a–f*). The stem stays upright – making the point that the appearance of a plant may be vastly altered by the stance of the limbs alone, though of course in life the stem itself might also contort. In *g*, *h* and *i*, stems and branches remain identical but the angles at which the leaves are held are radically altered, creating what might be three different species.

The way in which leaves are angled to the branch will also affect the working sequence: if they are more or less erect in relation to the stem (fig. 23*a*) it is easier to work from the lowest upwards, using the first as a guide for placing the others; if leaves are reflexed as in *b*, the upper ones determine the positions of the rest. Pairs of opposite leaves emerging from the stem at something like a right-angle are more clearly and pleasingly presented if shown as in *c* rather than as in *d*.

22 Posture: **a–f** effects of moving limbs through postures seen in nature; **g–i** different effects achieved by altering angles at which leaves are carried

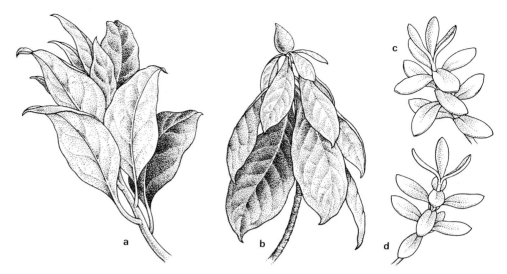

23 Leaf postures

LEAF ARRANGEMENTS Though there are ample botanical terms to describe the ways in which leaves are arranged upon stems, there are just a few basic themes, which allow great variation. Leaves may be *opposite*, *alternate*, *whorled* or *spiralled*; they may also be in groups or clumps – though even in the tightest grouping a definite pattern can usually be found.

Trichomes – hairs, bristles and prickles

Trichomes (fig. 24) are defined as outgrowths of the epidermis but this does not begin to suggest their beauty or interest. Botanically they may be categorized by structure, by density upon leaves, stems, petioles etc., and by size. For instance, a surface is *puberulous* when it is evenly covered (density) in hairs (structure) so minute (size) as to be just visible to the naked eye.

Problems often arise from trichome density, as when long erect hairs thickly cover a stem – a situation almost impossible to depict with accuracy in ink. A workable solution is merely to suggest them in a habit study (though still keeping the length and the posture correct) and to give more detail in an inset. (See also chapter 7 under *Dissections*.)

24 Trichome types (not to scale)

Trichomes range from simple single-celled hairs to the poisoned needle of the nettle, the thorn of the rose, and the elaborately sculpted leaf-scales of some rhododendrons. As always, watch for patterns – certain organs may carry hairs absent from other parts; there may be an admixture of various trichome types; hairs are sometimes organized in lines along mid-ribs, margins or from nodes.

A plant or part of a plant is described as *glabrous* where there are no hairs, and it is just as important to show this condition as it is to draw hairs where they are present. Be cautious – it is not uncommon for hairs to be invisible against some surfaces, only to be revealed by a raking side light as being present in some density.

Cactus spines have special characteristics. First, a warning: aside from the clear threat presented by large and often easily detached spines, watch out for the minute, sometimes almost microscopic spines known as *glochids*. For example, some species of *Opuntia* carry white to rust-coloured pads which are composed of aggregations of glochids – and even brushing against them can implant thousands of barbed darts which may cause severe irritation.

A spine-covered cactus may look baffling, but once you have understood the various patterns, the challenge is only to dexterity. In fig. 25 a step by step approach is shown which can be applied to many if not most, cactus species. First the overall shape *a* is worked out by ignoring the spines and examining the outline described by the raised *areoles* or *tubercles*. The way in which the areoles are disposed will help you to establish the foundation shown at *b*; loose to tight spirals will often be present as shown in the shaded areas. A count of the areoles visible along the shaded strips will ensure that the double spiral framework is accurate. The tubercles and areoles may then be drawn as at *c*. The numbers and types of spines present in each group, *d*, must be decided; there will often be a sequence from immature spines at the apex to a mature armature at a lower level. Finally, the spines are placed in perspective upon the understructure. Measurements are taken throughout as described on pp. 34–5. As may be seen from the sketch, any attempt to show a heavily armed cactus in detail in black ink would fail. White on black may be used as in scraper board, but the best approach is to use opaque pigments such as acrylics or gouache.

Surface ornament of stems and branches

Stems and branches have been mentioned in connection with posture and trichomes; now they are examined more closely. The term 'stem' is used here to include trunk, *rachis*, branch, branchlet etc. Variety is as wide for stem surfaces as it is for leaves; yet because the eye tends to be drawn to flowers and leaves, stems often receive less attention. This is especially so with trees, where foliage, flowers and fruit may be illustrated and distinctive bark designs ignored. Stems even of fleeting annual species carry patterns of pigmentation and/or structural developments such as fluting and keel-like projections.

Look for stem features such as buds (see p. 48), *leaf scars* and *lenticels* (fig. 26). Leaf scars often have quite specific shapes corresponding to the form of the petiole at the point of contact with the stem. Within the leaf scars,

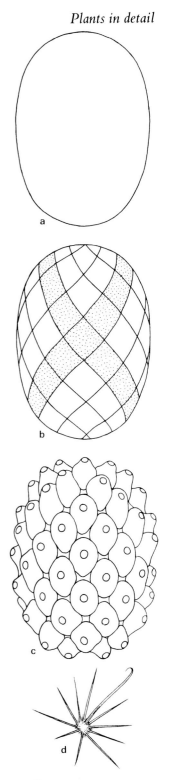

25 Cactus structure

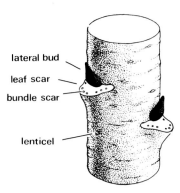

lateral bud

leaf scar

bundle scar

lenticel

26 Woody stem features

bundle scars may also be detected – these represent the *vascular* strands which pass up through the leaf petiole prior to leaf fall (*abscission*). Though often minute, the bundle scars (where visible) will be seen to have a definite arrangement. Terminal bud scales also leave characteristic scars. Lenticels are small spongy openings in surrounding impermeable tissue that allow interchange of gases between internal tissues and the atmosphere. They are often seen as lens-shaped markings, either parallel with the *axis* or placed horizontally. Frequently lighter in tone than their surrounds, they are often prominent on stems, though they may also be found on other plant parts. Lenticels may be of importance to the artist in three ways: they are likely to have a size, shape and colour consistent within a group; the surrounding tissue is often ridged or otherwise modified by their presence; and although lenticels are not usually orientated in distinct lines, spirals etc. their placement is only apparently random, as their overall distribution may contribute to characteristic stem patterns.

Some forms of stem ornamentation are shown in fig. 27 where, in the first three examples, the upper and lower cut surfaces help to reveal structure. Sometimes in a drawing the stem end is allowed to fade out; this can give a quite pleasing effect, but information of value and interest is lost.

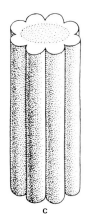

a   b   c   d   e

27 Stem ornamentation:
a, b flanges; **c** fluting;
d, e common bark types

Shading and the representation of surface markings on stems can suggest a surprising amount – certainly more than simply the direction of the light and the kind of ornamentation. It should be possible to indicate whether viewing is from above or below, whether the surface is receding from, or advancing towards the observer, and the rate at which this movement occurs, from a slow curve to a sharp kink. Changes in direction are more easily shown if the stem is seen from the side, but for a front or back view a technique for recording these effects is useful.

Even the smallest marks can be significant and, except where this would mislead, fortuitous markings which run counter to the trend should be omitted. Fig. 28 illustrates some of the possibilities. In *a*, the crudest drawing of a stem is shown – though further data could have been included by varying line strength etc. Here nothing more is implied than a straight smooth stem. The same parallel lines enclose the next three stems, yet by shading and directional trends indicated by lenticels and surface modelling

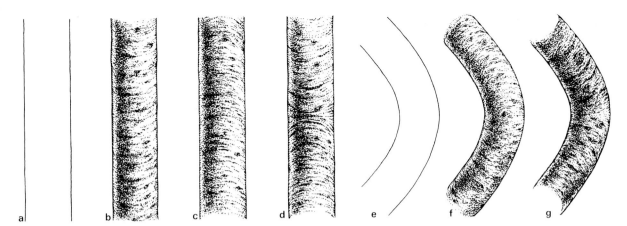

a   b   c   d   e   f   g

28 Shading and stem markings

it was easy to convey more information. In *b*, the stem is viewed from above, and in *c*, from below. When the two kinds of surface are placed together as in *d* it can be seen that they may be used to indicate an abrupt change of direction in the stem at around midpoint. This change could have been slowed by a less rapid move from one mode to the other. In a larger context, if *b* and *c* were portions of a plant shown in its entirety, the former might be seen as moving towards the viewer from the bottom to the top, and the latter from the top to the bottom.

Similar implications are made in the remaining stems: in fig. 28*e*, two lines illustrate a bend in one plane alone, yet the same lines in *f* and *g* give curves not only from top left to bottom right but also, respectively, forward and back.

Storage organs

Tubers, *bulbs* and *corms* are all food storage organs – adaptations of stems or leaves. The swollen petioles of plants such as celery and rhubarb function similarly. Enlarged stems of cacti and other succulents act as water reservoirs.

The *tunic*, the loose tissue surrounding a bulb or corm, will often appear almost as if woven, and an effort should be made to record the fibrous pattern. Some bulbs have membraneous translucent tissues which allow pigmentation to show through from one layer to another. Fig. 29*a* shows the way in which the tone of the colouring is modified where the tissues overlap. Layers wrap over each other in a particular sequence and this should be indicated wherever it is visible – sometimes the fine *hyaline* margins are impossible to pick out without dissection.

One characteristic common to all storage organs is dictated by their function – they are receptacles and so tend towards rotundity. In the potato form, fig. 29*b*, only preconception suggests that it is not discoid. Line thicknesses and directions in *c*, and a better choice of 'eye' placement, help to create the required effect, and with the addition of shading (*d*) plumpness results.

Look carefully at surface markings on storage organs – they may be the remnants of past processes, or precursors of coming events – as in the 'eyes' of the potato: these depressions, containing groups of buds, represent the axils of scale-like leaves and they are definite in structure.

45

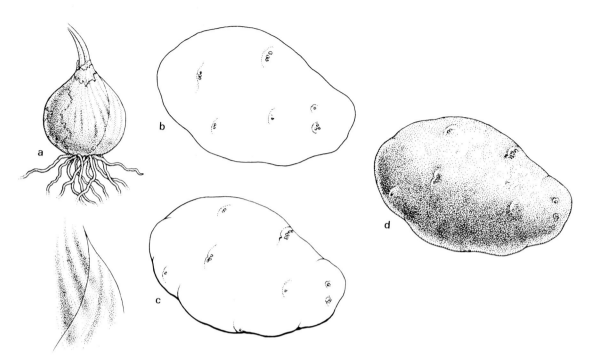

29 Storage organs: **a** bulb with detail showing overlapping translucent tissues; **b, c, d** indicating rotundity (see text)

Roots

When illustrating a whole plant, do not neglect the root system. Sometimes all species in a genus may have like roots and there would be small gain in showing them other than in perhaps one example. In other cases a portrayal of the underground parts may be of special interest.

Roots may be too long, massive or spreading to fit at anything like life-size on a plate. They then may be suggested with a minimum of detail at a reduced scale; treated diagrammatically; or photographed. Occasionally quite small plants will be found to possess extraordinarily long and spreading roots. It may be sensible in such instances to show the relationship between the parts above and below ground by an inset showing a much reduced outline of the entire plant. This will supplement the detail given in the body of the illustration where the roots may be shown as terminating abruptly in an artificial line.

As always, the first step is to try to understand what is happening – to analyse the underlying structure. Often this may be quite obscure even after all soil has been gently removed under running water. It is helpful to suspend the roots in water and view them through the walls of a glass container, but allowance should be made for the magnifying effect.

Up to this point mention of a specific medium has been avoided. Yet roots require a decision as to whether to work in pencil, ink, water-colour, gouache etc. as the medium modifies the method. The most difficult (though the most common) medium for this subject is ink. As it is used for so much scientific illustration, I am assuming here that the work is in this medium.

For present purposes I am also assuming that the subject has no definite, helpful form such as a single taproot or even an agglomeration of several large roots accompanied by subsidiaries, but consists of an amorphous fibrous mass. The difficulty is not just that of drawing the specimen accurately, which alone might be challenging enough, but also of presenting the information so that the reader may absorb it without becoming confused. Fig. 30 outlines procedure.

In *a* the overall dimensions of the root system are taken – note that the average length and width of the mass are the most useful, though the extremes are also recorded. Next, the appearance of a single root is examined (*b*): what is the thickness at the point of emergence? – does it branch? – do the branches themselves branch? – does it taper slowly or abruptly? – are root hairs prominent? – and so on.

At stage *c* several typical roots are pencilled lightly as a framework, showing thickness, length, number of branches, twists and turns, etc. They are then inked in, leaving small breaks where other roots cross them, to be filled in later. The upper sides of roots and lateral branches are inked first, then the remainder using the first lines as guides. Right-handed artists will find it easier to start with the left-hand line of vertical branches; for left-handers the reverse is true.

For step *d* the pencil is left aside; it would be time-consuming and of no value to attempt to draw the whole meandering tangle in both pencil and ink. As long as the roots are accurate in character it doesn't matter how they wander, and at this stage direct work with the pen is more appropriate. The specimen and the established guide roots are referred to constantly.

Watch for the moment when the addition of a few more lines would make the structure too dark and heavy. You will probably be aware of this well before the actual number of strands has been depicted. Then, as

30 Roots: sequence of drawing

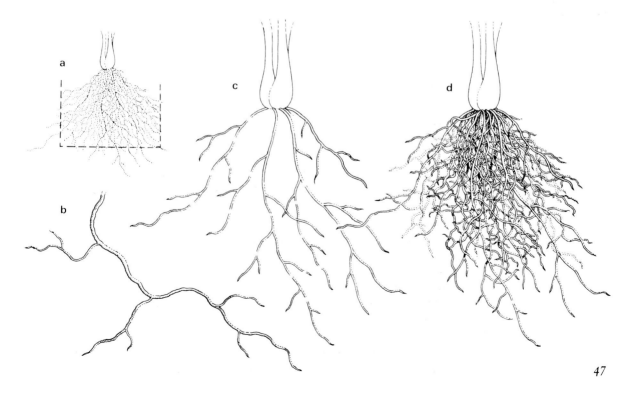

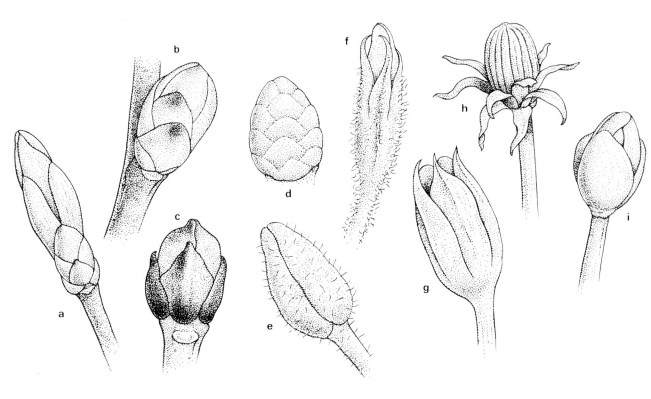

31 Buds: leaf buds –
a sycamore, *Acer
pseudoplatanus*; **b** hazel,
Corylus avellana; **c** ash,
Fraxinus excelsior; **d** oak,
Quercus robur. Flower buds
– **e** poppy, *Papaver* sp.;
f primrose, *Primula vulgaris*;
g foxglove, *Digitalis
purpurea*; **h** dandelion,
Taraxacum officinale; **i** lesser
celandine, *Ranunculus ficaria*

shown in *d*, the rest can be suggested by lighter broken and dotted lines. Finally, touches of shadow may be added: this should not be at random, but without misleading may be used to give a more pleasing aspect and greater clarity.

Buds

Buds may enfold developing leaves and/or flowers (fig. 31). Those which overwinter are insulated by scales which may be arranged in a variety of ways; in drawing them the patterns in which the scales fit together or overlap should be unravelled. With flower buds the emerging *corolla* will unfold in a particular style and often this will be suggested by the modelling of the bud at quite an early phase: a beautiful example of this is seen in *Kalmia*, mountain laurel, in which the smallest flower buds are distinctively spiralled; in contrast, the poppies, *Papaver* spp., appear to have their *petals* cramped into the enveloping *sepals* in an apparently haphazard way not indicated by the form of the developing bud. Where the *calyx* opens to expose the flower the lines along which opening will take place may be discernible and should be drawn.

Fruits

Here the term 'fruit' is used loosely, to include not only the ripe *ovary* or group of ovaries containing seeds but also the reproductive bodies of other groups of plants.

It is not always possible to show fruits, as plants are generally illustrated during flowering. Some species generously display flowers and fruits together, though more often this is not the case. Naturally both should not be shown on the same branch when this would not happen in life, though it is often worth reserving a portion of a plate to include the fruit later. It may be shown as an inset, or as one of several features surrounding a habit study; or perhaps a separate branch may be inserted at a later date (noted in the caption or text).

For convenience, fruits may be divided into broad and informal categories: dry – *follicles, capsules, nuts* etc., and wet – *drupes, berries, pomes* and so on. Dry fruits may be further subdivided into those that *dehisce* – peas, mustards, poppies etc., and those that are *indehiscent* – buttercups, grasses, walnuts etc. A selection is shown in fig. 32.

There are scores of botanical descriptive words for fruits and their parts in addition to those mentioned above, but they need not concern us here. But there are some non-specific factors to bear in mind for illustrating.

It is essential that the fruit should be mature – with familiars such as blackberries and strawberries the ripe and the unripe are easily distinguished, but with unfamiliar or exotic species maturity may not be so obvious. Sometimes the final phases of ripening bring about dramatic changes in appearance. Wherever unripe and ripe fruits occur together it may be appropriate to illustrate a sequence.

32 Several fruit types: **a** legume, *Sarothamnus*; **b** berry, *Lycopersicon*; **c** capsule, *Viola*; **d** capsule, *Papaver*; **e** schizocarp, *Myrrhis*; **f** schizocarp, *Acer*; **g** drupe, *Daphne*; **h** achene studded aggregate fruit, *Fragaria*; **i** follicle, *Aquilegia*; **j** nut (acorn), *Quercus*

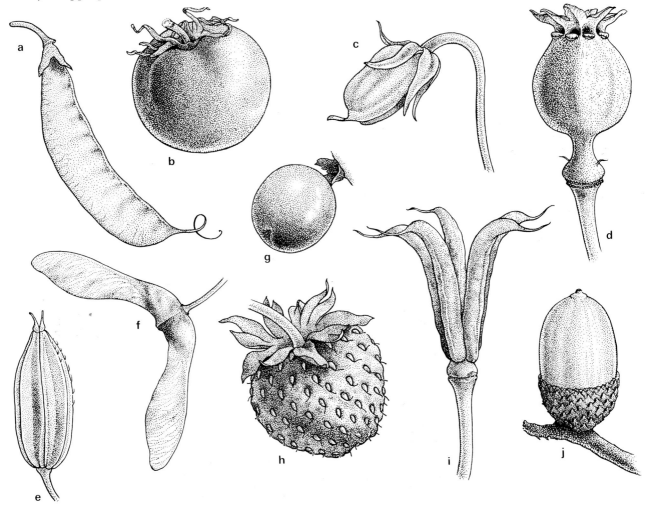

The methods by which seeds or spores are distributed are reflected in the structure of the fruits which carry them. It is often readily seen where seeds will be carried by the wind, as with the dandelion, or where the whole fruit will be windborne – the ash and the sycamore spread in this way. Succulent fruits carrying hard pips are generally distributed by birds and animals.

Some fruits show lines of dehiscence along which opening will occur. Watch for such lines, as they will be characteristic at least of the species involved; sometimes they remain indistinct up to the time of rupture, in other cases they may be obvious throughout development or on maturity. As noted earlier, mature fruits should be shown, but a later phase where they open to expose seeds may also be figured.

Many fruits have a spiralled structure similar to that shown in the cactus diagram, fig. 25. A common example is the strawberry, *Fragaria* spp., where the 'seeds' (achenes containing seeds) are studded upon the fleshy body in a spiralled arrangement. The unrelated pinecones and pineapples also share this feature. The spiral occurs throughout nature – in animals (think of shellfish) as well as plants and inanimate matter; the pattern is seen from the double helix of DNA to nebulae wheeling in space.

Seeds

Though the dissecting microscope is necessary for most seed illustration, seeds do range in size from tiny dust-like particles to those which may be examined with the hand-lens or the naked eye (fig. 33). Some are highly ornamented, and once again patterning tends to be characteristic and of significance botanically.

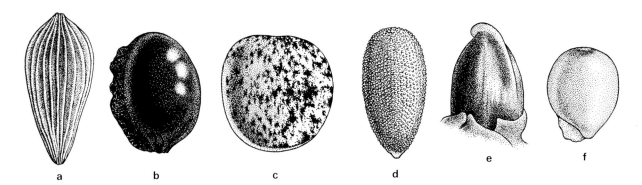

33 Seeds: **a** *Lactuca*;
b *Narcissus*; **c** *Vicia*;
d *Epilobium*; **e** *Dacrydium*;
f *Viola*

Bigger seeds usually have a fairly obvious morphology: it is the minute seed requiring microscopic examination that often provides a challenge. At a high level of magnification even the smallest seeds may reveal extraordinary surface sculpting – and this is best recorded by a scanning electron microscope (SEM). However, only the smallest detail need be treated in this way; the whole seed (of say 1 mm upwards) is still best handled by the artist as follows.

When selecting a seed for illustration you will see that examples vary as the parent plants do, and, although after examining twenty or thirty seeds it will be possible to see the 'ideal' approached in varying degrees by each, it will also usually be clear that no single seed is representative of the species. Often it will be possible to pick out from the sample many that will come close to the mean in shape and size; yet rarely will there be one among these that has in full all the characteristic marking and modelling present in some put aside as otherwise imperfect. In portraying one seed you will have to select from others to show all the important characters. One specimen might be typical in overall shape, yet the *papillae* may be obscure on part of the surface and this may be atypical, so this feature must be taken from another seed. Again, on the seed with perfect papillae their arrangement may break down – longitudinal lines may merge or be distorted in a fashion seen only in a few, and perhaps papillae at the base and apex of the seed may be less enlarged than in their fellows – so other seeds will be chosen for these qualities. In this way you can make a kind of amalgam that will come close to the truth, whereas a single electron micrograph cannot entirely succeed.

There are three main considerations in illustrating seeds and other minutiae: first, as noted above, representative characteristics must be defined and selected. Second, measurements from the micrometer eyepiece scale in the microscope must be taken with scrupulous accuracy: a 0.1 mm error is significant when scaled up in drawing a subject only 1 mm in length. Third, extra care has to be taken over the placement of lighting – for example, longitudinal corrugations seem to all but disappear from a seed coat when the light source is placed towards top or bottom (fig. 34).

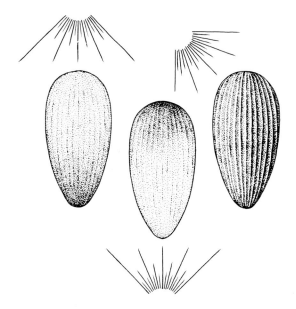

34 The effect of light placement in obscuring or revealing details of seeds

Flowers

A complete survey of flowers would fill volumes. Here I will simply define what a flower is, with a diagram of a 'typical' form with parts named, as this elementary botanical information is a must to any aspiring illustrator from the beginning. Next, a few useful categories of flowers will be noted, and types for these groupings will be illustrated and discussed.

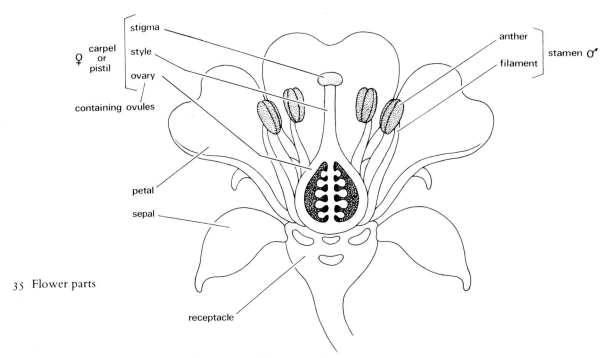

carpel or pistil ♀

stigma

style

ovary

containing ovules

petal

sepal

anther

filament

stamen ♂

35 Flower parts

receptacle

A concise definition of the term *flower* appears in *Biology of Plants*: 'The reproductive structure of angiosperms; a complete flower includes calyx, corolla, androecium (stamens), and gynoecium (carpels), but all contain at least one stamen or one carpel' (fig. 35).

For the botanical artist flowers may be divided into two main categories: *actinomorphic* (*radially symmetrical* or *regular*) – where the petals radiate from the centre of the flower and are more or less equidistant each from the other; and *zygomorphic* (*bilaterally symmetrical* or *irregular*) – flowers that may be divided into two like-parts along only one plane (see fig. 36). A few groups have flowers that are not divisible into like-parts.

The above concepts are useful to remember as they affect dissections, methods of measurement etc. The botanist uses a host of other descriptive floral terms and these are also needed by the artist who wishes to communicate fluently. In addition to knowing something of floral parts it is also helpful to be able to recognize the various modes in which the flowers are arranged on the stems, the *inflorescences*. There is no great gain in describing inflorescence types in detail here though an exception can be made for the *capitulum*.

In essence a capitulum is a tight inflorescence of usually *sessile* (stalkless) flowers which are of two kinds: *ray florets* and *disc florets*, the former being disposed about the perimeter of the latter (fig. 37). This type of inflorescence is commonly met with, as it is present in the enormous *family* Asteraceae (Compositae, composites). Though inappropriate in a biological sense, it is logical in terms of form to place composite capituli here with actinomorphic flowers.

Oddly, this apparently simple composite form is not easy to draw well. As demonstrated in fig. 38 there are several difficulties. One is that identified in the fungi (fig. 15), of sitting the heads upon the stems convincingly, which is solved by projecting the line of the stem through the capitulum

(*a*). The next stage is to put in the massed disc florets in outline (*d–g*). These often describe a dome, though the centre may be somewhat flat or even concave. These features break down into an arrangement of ellipses which must be placed in correct relationship. The key ellipse is that at the base of the 'dome', where the disc florets meet the *receptacle* hidden beneath; once this is correctly sited the rest follow.

36 Flower examples.
Zygomorphic –
a *Cypripedium*; **b** *Digitalis*;
c *Mimulus*; **g** *Delphinium*.
Actinomorphic –
d *Aquilegia*; **e** *Rosa*;
f *Geranium*; **h** *Meconopsis*

37 Generalized structure of a capitulum

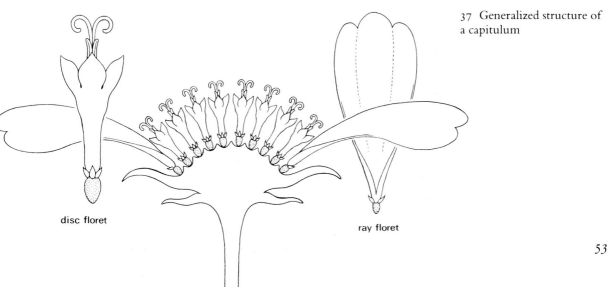

disc floret

ray floret

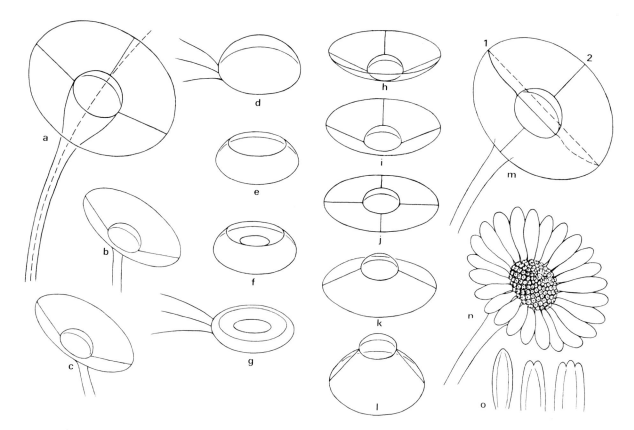

38 Drawing composite flower heads: **a** correctly sited head; **b, c** incorrectly sited heads (exaggerated); **d–g** generalized outlines of disc florets; **h–l** generalized outlines of ray florets; **m** key lines in drawing a capitulum; **n** generalized head showing disc florets and radiating ray florets; **o** ray floret apices

The ellipse of the ray floret tips is rarely in the same plane as the ellipse at the base of the disc florets. The ray florets may form a saucer-shape or even a flask-shape (according to how far open they are) through all degrees of concavity from deep to shallow, until, when the rays are horizontal, the 'flower' becomes discoid; from that point the form becomes convex – through inverted saucer to inverted flask (*h–l*). Throughout this range there are just two key lines: the first describes the angle of the ray florets in relation to the disc, and the second depends upon the placement of the 'flower' in relation to the viewer – this was established in drawing the ellipse at the base of the disc florets. For clarity these two lines are shown in fig. 38*m*, with the lines that follow indicated by dashes.

Once the framework is established the ray florets may be drawn in and the disc details added. Remember that, as with the mushroom gills, the outer florets radiate from a central point. They also may overlap in layers, and some may bend away from the others. Note the ray floret tips – they are frequently divided and these divisions can affect the modelling of the floret surface.

A spiralled arrangement of disc florets is often evident, especially in larger heads. This may be distinct when the ray florets are in bud, but the pattern can be confused as they open. In some plants such as the big sunflowers, *Helianthus* spp., the spirals are striking, though even in the common (English) daisy, *Bellis perennis*, the same arrangement may be picked out.

The completed drawing in fig. 38*n* shows the character of the flower-head insofar as the upper parts are exposed, yet the receptacle, hidden in this case, may also be of importance. It is often covered by *phyllaries* (*bracts*) which are disposed and ornamented variously. As with all flower illustration, a range from 'flower'-bud to fruiting-head should be shown where this is feasible.

The next flower, alkanet, *Pentaglottis sempervirens* (fig. 39) is also actinomorphic – the same principles are involved as in the composite flower, though here their application is more straightforward. At the centre of the lobes of the *corolla* is a dark orifice or throat, and this is the point from which the drawing should originate. It is placed along the line of the projected stem (*pedicel* in this case) and from it the length of a non-foreshortened lateral lobe is taken, to set the limits for the broad ellipse which defines the flower outline. Here the corolla lobes fuse towards the flower centre (see p. 57). Lines radiating from this centre follow the twists of the corolla lobes and intersect the outer ellipse at almost equidistant points. The flower is placed so that a portion of the densely hairy calyx and pedicel may be seen.

The *Iris* (fig. 40) is another actinomorphic flower, though contrasting strongly with the two previous examples. The snag here for the novice is that this kind of flower appears at first to be a jumble of disparate parts, though on analysis only three units are found and these are each in triplicate. The example on the right has been 'exploded' to show the components clearly: *a*, is the *standard*; *b*, the *fall*; *c*, the *petaloid style*-branch. Flowers that appear intricate should always be dissected or gently unravelled to expose their workings.

Though the flowers in fig. 40 resemble each other, two different species

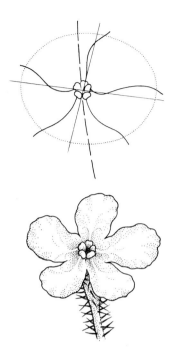

39 Actinomorphic flower: alkanet, *Pentaglottis sempervirens*

40 Actinomorphic flower: *Iris*, structure

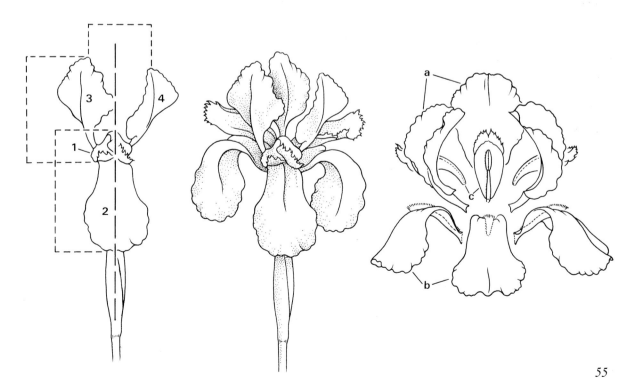

are represented; from this you will see that once the basic components and the way in which they fit together are assimilated, you can then decode other species in this genus. If the *Iris* flower is looked at with the foregoing in mind, a working sequence will resolve itself. This is shown in the diagram at the left. The first proposition is that the flower is balanced along a vertical axis (indicated by the heavy broken line). Next it can be seen that the unit to start on is comprised of the components numbered 1 and 2 on the diagram – the petaloid stigma and the fall. Once these are drawn, the two standards (3 and 4) can be erected, and, remembering the lessons of the fungus (pp. 33–6), the rest may be completed confidently – using the established parts as guides. Important dimensions are indicated by dotted lines on the sketch and it may be helpful to take others. Decorative markings have been left off for this exercise as they would have obscured the forms. Whatever the medium used, the characteristic pigmented venation would be added in the later phases of the study.

The iris in fig. 40 was orientated for ease of explanation; in an actual plate it would be useful to show at least one bloom with one of the standards more or less facing the front so that the base of the flower, in *Iris* the *spathe valves*, would be seen.

The next subject (fig. 41) is a zygomorphic (irregular) flower from the Papilionaceae – like Compositae, one of the largest of the families of flowering plants. The bilateral symmetry of this form is not helpful unless the flower is facing you – then measurements are more easily made and proportions assessed. In illustrating an inflorescence of this pea-type plant a bloom thus orientated may be included to show the standard complete, but the full-frontal position is usually not ideal in that much is obscured.

41 Zygomorphic flower: broom, *Sarothamnus* cultivar – **a** lateral view; **b** three-quarter view; **c** exploded view of parts

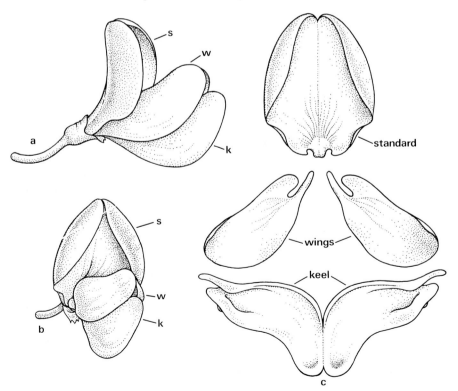

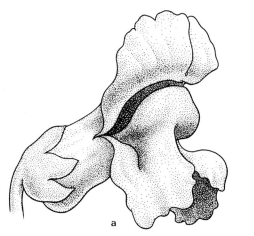
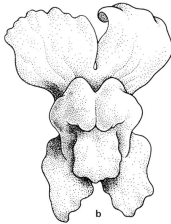

a   b

Often an inflorescence can be placed to show flowers from various angles, including a hind view.

Apart from the hidden sex organs, this flower, like the iris, breaks down into three components, known as the *standard*, the *wings* and the *keel*. Though the parts may vary in size they will still be recognized in common plants such as peas, beans, clovers, vetches, brooms etc.

Bilateral symmetry along a vertical axis is evident when zygomorphic flowers are viewed from the front, but the same flowers seen from the side are generally aligned obliquely or diagonally. This side view is often difficult to draw as appropriate measuring points tend to be placed at angles to the axis, and these angles may be awkward to estimate with accuracy. Dimensions should be taken where possible but with zygomorphic flowers a good eye is especially valuable.

An oblique posture is also seen in the snapdragon, *Antirrhinum* sp. (fig. 42); in this flower the corolla is fused into a tube without separate parts (*gamopetalous* – with the petals united, at least at the base – as distinct from *polypetalous*, where the petals are entirely separated). Though the parts are united, this does not inhibit variety; the families and genera that have flowers of this kind – the mints, sages, lavenders, foxgloves, pentstemons etc. – testify to this.

Gamopetaly and polypetaly are found in both actinomorphic and zygomorphic flowers. The two modes are of botanical significance so you should try to show the points at which the petals unite; and to make it clear if they do not. Naturally this applies not only to petals but also to calyces and all other parts that may or may not fuse.

In the snapdragon, the lower lip of the 'dragon's mouth' provides a good example of *inflation*. Many flowers possess this feature to some degree; sometimes the shapes do resemble inflated bladders or sacs, more often they appear as if moulded over a three-dimensional form.

The final zygomorphic flower for discussion is from the family Orchidaceae – which consists of some 17,000 species. Depending upon who is doing the counting, this is either the second or third largest family of the *angiosperms* (flowering plants). A knowledge of the parts of the orchid flower will help you to recognize the basic structures, in spite of their many cryptic and flamboyant forms.

42 Zygomorphic flower: snapdragon, *Antirrhinum* cultivar, **a** lateral and **b** frontal views

Walter Fitch, after illustrating at least six volumes of works on the family, speaks with authority: 'Perhaps there are no flowers more varied in size, form, and colour, than those of orchids, and I think I may add more difficult to sketch, if the artist has not some general knowledge of their normal structure . . . Indeed they almost seem to have been created to puzzle botanists, or to test an artist's abilities, and consequently they are all the more worthy of a skilful pencil in endeavouring to do justice to them . . . It is impossible to lay down any rules for sketching these protean plants, but if the structure is not correctly rendered in a drawing it is worse than useless, as no colouring will redeem it.' (From articles in *The Gardeners' Chronicle*, 1869.)

To help you understand the drawing of an orchid flower in fig. 43 a botanical description is useful. 'In the orchids, the three carpels are fused, and, as in the composites, the ovary is inferior. Unlike the composites, however, each ovary contains many thousands of minute ovules; consequently each pollination event may result in the production of a very large number of seeds. Usually only one stamen is present (in the lady's slipper orchids, there are two), and this is characteristically fused with the style and stigma into a single complex structure, the column. The entire contents of the anther are held and distributed as a unit, the pollinium. The three petals are modified so that the two lateral ones form wings and the third forms a cuplike lip that is often very large and showy. The sepals, also three in number, are often coloured and petal-like in appearance. The flower is also irregular.' (Raven, Evert and Curtis, *Biology of Plants*.)

In spite of Fitch's strictures, a few general indications should nevertheless prove worth while.

Most orchids show the double 'Y' pattern seen in fig. 43, though in some this design is almost completely hidden. The double 'Y' is formed

43 Zygomorphic flower: generalized orchid structure – frontal and lateral views; inset demonstrates the establishment of a 'ruffled' margin

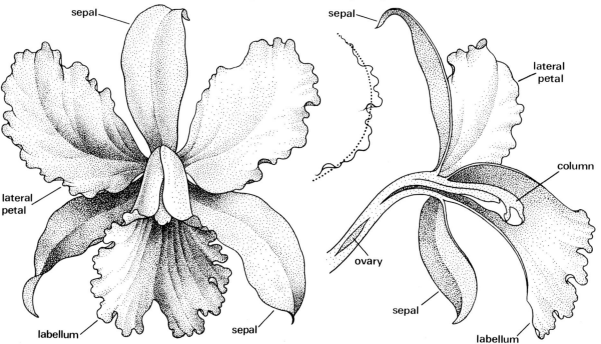

by the way in which the petals and sepals are arranged – a 'Y' is described by the lateral petals and the *labellum* or lip, and this is imposed upon the inverted letter form seen in the sepals. This formation is also clear in numerous other *monocotyledonous* species.

In an actual illustration, for better information and for aesthetic appeal it is usual to site subjects in a three-quarter view, tilted left or right. However, the frontal view shown here demonstrates the 'Y' forms well, and also suggests that the sequence to be followed in working on flowers of this kind is really closely related to that described for the iris. The key dimension here is from the apex of the labellum to the base. Once this petal is established, the tip of the *column* should be accurately placed and further dimensions taken from this point. The two lateral petals should be drawn after the labellum, and these three elements will serve as guides for the positioning of the sepals.

Do not be misled by the undulate margins of the petals (or similar features in other flowers). In wandering along such a complex outline one tends to stray from the main route: as for leaves, the solution is lightly to pencil in an approximate margin before tackling the frills in detail.

Many species in this family show all but incredible designs. Their bizarre formations earn orchids such epithets as 'man', 'monkey', 'lizard', 'bee', 'spider' etc.; this kind of patterning can help the artist by striking a responsive chord in his mind. It is surprising how much easier it becomes to draw a shape when you find something familiar in it.

Sex expression

Botanical illustrators often work mainly with flowering plants, though most will also make excursions into the *gymnosperms* (pines etc.) and other groups on occasion. It is therefore appropriate to look specifically at reproductive organs in angiosperm flowers.

The sexual organs of flowers show almost as much variety of form and colour as the corollas that enfold them. Their characteristic disposition is also of fundamental interest to the botanist, in spite of John Ruskin's admonition: 'With these obscene processes and prurient apparitions the gentle and happy scholar of flowers has nothing whatever to do.' (*Proserpina*, 1874–86)

In thinking about male and female parts of the flower it is useful to absorb several terms. In fig. 35 the male organs, the *stamens*, surround the female organ, the *carpel* or *pistil* (single in this instance, but commonly – as in buttercups – present in numbers). The male organs are known collectively as the *androecium*, 'house of man', and the carpel or carpels as the *gynoecium*, 'house of woman'. Flowers containing stamens and carpels are termed *perfect*. Sometimes either stamens or carpels are absent and the flower is *imperfect* and either *staminate* or *carpellate*. Various sexual groupings are described by a complicated terminology.

The way in which the stamens and carpels are situated in relation to each other, and to the surrounding floral envelope, is important. In flowers with few stamens and carpels, any errors in their placing would be glaring to the informed eye. Where stamens and carpels are numerous (as in roses) it is often possible to pick out spiralled or whorled arrangements. Occasionally the siting of male and female parts will be puzzling, as in the Orchidaceae and Stylidiaceae where *anthers* and *stigmas* are borne on a single column; but more often the structures will be quite distinct.

Stamens (fig. 44a–d) consist of two portions: the anther bearing pollen in sacs (one to four in number) is carried on a *filament* (stalk). In addition to the size and shape of the anther, you should also try to show the way in which it dehisces to expose the pollen grains. Most anthers split longitudinally (b), though some have other modes – in *Rhododendron*, for instance, twin apical pores open (c) allowing pollen to spill out in viscid strands.

Anthers pose three small problems: first, they often shrink drastically as they open, and so wherever practicable some should be shown unopened. Second, in different breeding systems anthers open before, at the same time as, or after the stigma becomes receptive. This sometimes means that a choice has to be made between mature anthers or mature stigmas. With inflorescences it may be that a sequence of development will be apparent. The third point about anther dehiscence is that the process is often initiated by a change from moist outside air to the dry air of the studio.

Anthers are fixed to filaments in two ways: they may be *basifixed* with the anther sitting on top of the filament (a); or they may be *dorsifixed* with the filament attached to the 'back' of the anther (b) – the anther may then be *versatile* and swing freely, or it may be held rigid. Anthers are seldom highly ornamented though they may have spurs or projections as in *Euphrasia*. Sometimes they are joined at their margins to form a cylinder or ring.

Relative to the size of the flower, anther filaments show a huge range in length: in wind-pollinated plants such as grasses, and many common tree species of temperate zones, the anthers hang on long filaments well clear of the rest of the flower; in other species with different methods of pollination, filaments may barely be visible; in some families (Leguminoseae, Malvaceae) they may be united for at least part of their length to form a tube. Watch for the characteristic curves that filaments describe, they are often of subtlety and beauty.

Filament cross-sections range from cylindrical to more or less strap-shaped; filaments of the former type are usually rigid or springy whereas the latter may be flaccid. In dissections it is important to show the points from which the filaments arise: for instance, where the stamens appear in two distinct sets – one set emerging above the other in the *floral tube*; they may also emerge from the same level but be different in length – a longer set from between the petals and a shorter one from each petal base. Many other kinds of arrangements are seen. Sometimes filaments will carry hairs, especially towards the base (d).

The female flower parts, the gynoecium, may, as shown in fig. 35, be a single basic unit, a carpel, though the carpels may also be paired, or they may be several to numerous. Where present in numbers, they may be spirally arranged (fig. 44e) or whorled. Each carpel consists of three parts: stigma, *style*, and *ovary*. The ovary eventually becomes the fruit, or a section of a composite fruit, and it contains one to many *ovules* which ripen into seeds.

The stigma is composed of specialized tissues, often with minute papillae

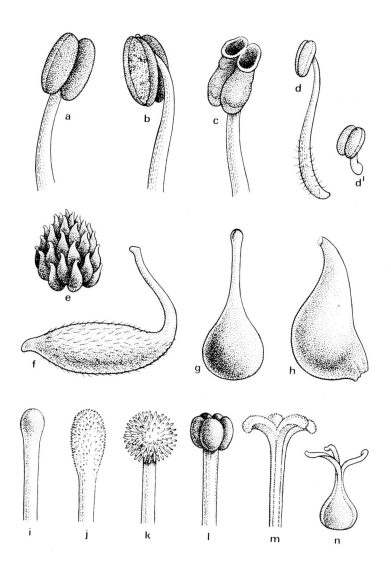

and/or sticky exudates, which capture pollen, initiating fertilization. A stigma may be little more than a moist swelling at the apex of the style or it may be lobed, branched or otherwise elaborated. Often the structures are of the greatest interest to the *taxonomist* and slight variations may be helpful in defining species. Some stigma types are shown in fig. 44 *i–m*.

The style is an outgrowth of tissue from the ovary, bearing the stigma at its apex. It may be an unbranched column, or variously branched as in fig. 44*n*; it is sometimes poorly differentiated (*h*) or even absent – the stigma then rests upon the ovary and is termed sessile. The style may be upright in relation to the ovary, or it may be flexed into one of several positions. It may be constant in position throughout development or it may change markedly to thrust the stigma into place for pollination, lengthening quickly as the stigma matures; sometimes it is angled to one side, or *reflexed* to avoid self-pollination. Or, if self-pollination is the mode,

44 Sexual structures (representative forms): **a–d** stamens; **e–h** carpels; **i–m** stigmas; **n** composite ovary with partially fused styles

the style will be of a length to allow the stigma contact with the anthers within the same floral envelope.

Even within one species there may be several different pollination stratagems. Where this is so it is often feasible to show the range – depending upon the purpose of the illustration. It may also be useful to do this where, as mentioned above, there is a distinct developmental sequence.

Ovaries, fig. 44 *e–h*, enclose the ovules (potential seeds) and so are variously container-shaped. An ovary may be simple or derived from several fused carpels. In the latter form, the styles also may have fused for all their length, as indicated by lobing of the stigmatic area and fluting of the column (*l,m*). In other cases each fused element of a composite ovary may retain its separate style, or the styles may be fused in part (*n*). Often the composite condition is also suggested by markings or modelling of the ovary itself. Ovaries may carry various surface ornamentations as well as hairs and other trichomes.

The arrangement of ovules within ovaries is botanically important, but the topic is complex and for information the interested reader should consult more specialized texts.

The position of the ovary in relation to the disposition on the floral axis of the other flower parts is important. The ovary is *superior* (fig. 35) when it is attached to the receptacle above the sepals, petals and stamens; it is *inferior* (fig. 67c) when it is attached below these parts. (In the former condition the flower is termed *hypogynous*; in the latter the flower is *epigynous*. A third form is recognized where a cup-shaped extension of the receptacle will bear petals and stamens about its rim above the superior ovary – this type of flower is known as *perigynous*.) Each mode should be visible in an illustration when it is clearly seen in a flower: it is easy to allow a superior ovary to be obscured by petals, but if one bloom is slightly inclined, the position of the ovary becomes obvious. Inferior ovaries may be hidden by enveloping foliage – as in some evening primrose (*Oenothera*) species where the floral tube is long and often greenish towards the base, so that in both form and colour it may resemble a *peduncle* (flower stalk) and the point where the often not strongly differentiated ovary is reached may be well down among leaves.

In the definition of a flower on p. 52 it was stated that all contain at least one stamen *or* one carpel, indicating that some flowers may be male and others female; yet the situation is more complicated than this. Some species display both male and female parts, yet are functionally either male *or* female. In these the non-functional organs (sometimes partially functional) may be smaller in size than their fully functional counterparts, or may be absent altogether, or be much reduced or otherwise modified in form – as in *staminodes* (sterile stamens or structures resembling them). The above possibilities give rise to complex situations where diverse breeding systems may operate within a single species or even within a population.

The calyx is the outermost whorl of the floral envelopes; it may appear quite separate (sometimes green and leaf-like) and be indistinctly to distinctly lobed – the lobes being known as sepals; or it may not be clearly differentiated from the rest of the *perianth* (the calyx and corolla together) in which case each unit of the perianth is referred to as a *tepal*. A distinct calyx is shown in fig. 42. In the orchid (fig. 43) the sepals of the calyx are petaloid – in some flowers the sepals equal the petals in showiness. Sometimes the sepals may be the more visible structures, with the petals being reduced, as in *Delphinium* where petals are negligible. There is often a pattern of calyx lobing – one lobe may be longer than the rest, two may be placed close together, or there may be other arrangements. The placement of the calyx lobes in relation to the petals should also be noted.

Glands within the flower (or, in some species, on other parts of the plant body) that secrete nectar, *nectaries*, are occasionally large enough to be shown, particularly if the subject is being drawn at larger than life-size (fig. 45). Excess nectar should be removed if the form of the nectary is obscured.

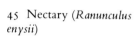

45 Nectary (*Ranunculus enysii*)

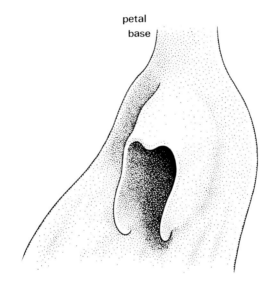

petal
base

Though the foregoing should help you when working upon mainstream subjects, you are sure to come across forms not covered here – even the most extraordinary cannot be excluded. Space precludes a treatment of grasses (Gramineae): though also flowering plants, they have a separate vocabulary of terms, more particularly for their floral parts; but the principles outlined here, with additional guidance from a volume such as C. E. Hubbard's *Grasses*, should help you to achieve a working knowledge.

6 Pencil

When plants are to be drawn in black and white, the main choices for media are ink, scraper board or pencil. Any of these media are suitable for reproduction by photolithography (offset lithography) which is the process now used for almost all printed books – although there can be a slightly greying effect in the reproduction if printing is not of a high standard. For letterpress reproduction, ink or scraper board drawings are usually more suitable.

A printing process known as 'duo-tone', which often gives a single-colour enrichment in reproductions of photographs, may also be used with fine effect for reproducing pencil drawings, when cost or other considerations prohibit the use of full colour.

Though work in pencil may be suitable for much scientific illustration in its ability to record minute elements and to give a full tonal range, the use of ink is so entrenched in this field that pencil tends to be reserved for less formal use – interpretative guide books, etc. For these purposes pencil is often an excellent choice: though its capacity is in fact greater than ink, it suggests a softer, more relaxed approach. But once you have explored the techniques of both media, you will find that a skilled pencil study may demand more work than a similar drawing in ink, because it is possible to reveal a wholly different level of detail. Where a slightly sketchy style is suitable, pencil is again ideal.

Equipment

PENCILS are graded from 6H, hard and light in tone, to 1H, then HB, and through the Bs to 6B which is soft and black. There is no hard black pencil in the above range; and though hard black pencils are available outside the H and B designations, those I have used have had waxy substances in their makeup which render them almost non-erasable. A compromise has often to be made: fine details require a hard point maintained for a reasonable period, and a drawing with a broad tonal range will require strong blacks in shadowed areas. The obvious solution is to use several grades of pencil; but work done with a soft pencil smears easily – and in a detailed drawing this may be disastrous. A fixative spray prevents smudges, but in tonal illustrations as described below the option of erasure must be retained to the finish; and, since also commercial fixatives cannot be guaranteed against eventual discoloration or other undesirable behaviour, their use is not recommended for any work where the subject matter may be of lasting importance.

How, then, is an unsmudged drawing obtained? First, by using pencils from around the middle part of the range – I find an HB the best; second, by ensuring that when the work is stored it is protected at least by tissue paper; third, by making sure that in storage there is no lateral or rubbing movement. Folders are helpful (see chapter 12).

The ordinary HB pencil can achieve minute detail and subtle effects when used on a suitable paper. It does not smear over-easily and a point may be retained for a useful time. Its one disadvantage is that it cannot produce a deep velvety black.

All pencils should conform to the grade stamp they carry – marks made by one category should be consistent and should remain distinct from those made by the other grades. In general this is the case, though brands may differ slightly in the depth of 'blackness' obtainable, and occasionally a gritty texture is found in the lead – where this occurs the pencil is best discarded.

The pencil must be kept sharp, which means constant trimming and consequently a short life, especially if it is discarded as soon as it is too short to rest comfortably in the fold between the thumb and first finger. A pencil-extender (fig. 46) allows a pencil to be used to within the final inch of its length. So far I have not been able to find this device for sale in Britain (I have one of German make, bought in the United States), but it could be improvised from a tube of springy metal split partly up one side to allow a pencil to be inserted.

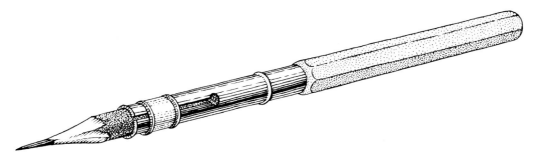

Although many people prefer a mechanical device for sharpening pencils, I would recommend a craft knife with changeable blades. For economy, the blade can be kept keen-edged with a fine-grained sharpening stone.

46 A pencil extender

Some believe that a pencil should be sharpened to a chisel-shaped tip, but I prefer a long point; this may be touched up numerous times before it becomes necessary to cut into the wood again (fig. 47). A long lead also

47 Pencil sharpened as described in text

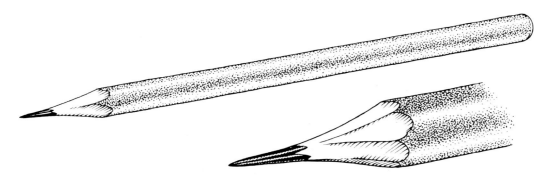

allows good visibility around the point. A piece of emery paper may be used to re-point pencils, but it tends to become a graphite reservoir to mark everything around.

PAPER Suitable paper is at least as important, perhaps even more so, than the right pencil. For a detailed plant portrait, the surface should be smooth, and not only in appearance – test it by rubbing an HB pencil over a small area, and if the grain or texture of the paper shows as in fig. 48 then the surface is unsatisfactory. On the other hand it may be so smooth and hard that the graphite particles are not retained; though the mark made may be uniform throughout, it will also be light in tone and however hard the lead is pressed against the surface, nothing beyond a mid-grey will result. Also undesirable is a soft slightly textured paper that may be flattened by hard pressure but will still allow texture to show through medium or light pressure.

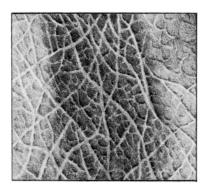 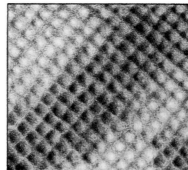 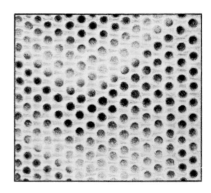

48 Pencil used on textured papers (an HB simulation of highly magnified surfaces)

The perfect surface is one that will absorb a maximum amount of graphite with a reasonable pressure; it should also be strong enough to remain intact after fairly vigorous use of a soft eraser.

Thickness or weight is a matter of individual preference; the paper should not be so thin as to cockle or deform when working over it, though it may be as thick as the heaviest board if you prefer. The heavier papers or boards are expensive.

Colour, although the least important factor, is worth consideration: for most botanical work you will find that glaring white is best avoided; given other essential qualities, the ideal is faintly off-white with a hint of warmth rather than tending towards the blue end of the spectrum.

The final criterion is that of durability. Paper should be made of rag; a wood based paper will discolour in time, and this process can be rapid with exposure to bright light.

ERASERS An eraser should be selected with care. Some which perform perfectly on one type of surface may leave ugly smears or be less effective on others. The use of two erasers (or more) is recommended – one should be fairly soft, yielding elastically and very slightly under firm finger pressure; the other hard and abrasive, yet not gritty or capable of leaving scratches. For the former kind a plastic eraser is ideal – it is uniform in texture with no small air-spaces or lumps (important for reasons explained below). In use it should not crumble, as the old-style gum eraser does; small particles should aggregate in rubbing to form spindle-shaped rolls which can be cleanly swept away, leaving no fine specks to catch under the pencil lead. Before any rubbing-out, always clean off the eraser by applying it to a sheet of spare paper.

FEATHER Using the eraser for white-line (see below) and for removing guide-lines or other unwanted material may produce a lot of debris. Blowing will remove only the larger particles, sweeps of a brush or hand may smudge – and the hand can leave traces of perspiration and/or oil. A couple of flicks with a feather will remove all crumbs without detrimental effect to either drawing or paper. A strong wing-pinion from a big bird such as a goose, swan or turkey will last for years in daily use. A wing feather is rather better than one from the tail, as the pinnules along the leading edge, being shorter, are more rigid than those of the trailing surface and so can be used when an occasional stubborn fragment resists removal. Nevertheless a handsome tail feather is not to be sneezed at. A dark feather is preferable to a light one as the latter will pick up a grey cast – though this washes off to some extent.

Equipment for general use as outlined in chapter 2 will also be needed when making pencil drawings.

Techniques
To reduce the risk of smudging, and to avoid transferring other substances to the work, a sheet of paper, of the same quality as that being drawn on, should always be between the hand and the actual working surface. As well as absorbing sweat and grease it serves as a useful area on which to try out a newly-sharpened lead or tricky shading. The best size for this sheet seems to be about 20 × 15 cm (8 × 6 in.); anything much smaller does not protect a large enough area, and a larger piece tends to blot out too much.

There are two basic ways of using a pencil – to make a line, or to make an area of tone.

LINE Before you start a drawing in line, a few preliminary strokes (fig. 49) will accustom your hand to the feel of the pencil and allow some appreciation of the qualities of the graphite line.

The pencil lines in the figure were drawn freehand without independent movement of the fingers or wrist. It is infinitely less cramping and tension-inducing to draw all lines, no matter how short, by movements originating from the shoulder or elbow, rather than from the wrist or fingers. You will find that long lines flow much better and even minute ones, such as those describing hairs, are not demanding when drawn in this way. The pencil should rest easily in the hand without the fingers being clenched.

Beyond a certain line length, varying with the individual, the whole arm becomes involved. Few are capable of completing very long lines accurately with single strokes; it is necessary to continue in a number of

49 'Doodling', exploring effects in pencil *line*: tonal variations achieved by changes in line-spacing and/or fluctuations in pressure on the pencil

comfortable movements. Each completed long line should have at least the *appearance* of resulting from one sure stroke.

The lines in fig. 49 are slightly uneven. Freehand work retains an organic or natural feeling – a vastly different quality from that of lines drawn with a set square or ruler. These aids should be reserved for diagrams, where a mechanical feeling is often an advantage.

When long lines, or a series of short ones, are drawn, the pencil blunts fairly quickly. The process is slowed noticeably by slowly rotating the pencil shaft in the hand to allow a new part of the graphite to touch the paper every so often. As the pencil is held at an angle, this gives an almost self-pointing action.

In a drawing done in line alone, the keynote should be simplicity, with an emphasis on qualities of tonal range (within the line) and delicacy. The line-drawing of the dog rose, *Rosa canina*, fig. 50, demonstrates something of these aspects, while falling short in other regards.

The procedure was basically that described on pp. 33–6. The drawing was started with the group of stigmas seen at the centre of the flower; with this established, the first key dimension was the rear petal, estimated by eye since the distance from stigmas to petal-tip would have been distorted by foreshortening. This petal was lightly drawn in before following with the other four, beginning with the one on the left, for which a measurement was taken with dividers as the apex of the petal fell in virtually the same plane as the stigmas. Especial care was taken with the foreshortened petal at the bottom left of the flower: it is difficult to resist the inclination to draw any foreshortened object as it would appear without the distortion due to perspective; here I was tempted to show the vertical distance between the base of the stigmas and the base of the petal as my intelligence insisted was correct, rather than as my eye saw it. It is a help to think momentarily of such forms as being abstract and without a third dimension. Again, it is useful to relate a puzzling object to adjacent forms that pose no problems; in this instance it is clear that the base of the petal does not extend as far down as the base of the dominant leaf on the far right.

The leaves were first drawn in as barely visible generalized outlines which were used as guides for the serrations before being removed by a gentle touch of the eraser.

The whole drawing was completed in outline before any parts were given emphasis. At that point the study was even in tone and dull in appearance. The final stage of a line drawing can be gratifying: the ground work is complete and all that remains is to give a feeling of life and interest by subtle additions. Here strengthening of the veins about the midribs indicates a light source from about the top right; this impression is re-inforced by minute dark areas under the flower and a darkening of the left side of the stem.

There are at least two weak points: the first (which could easily have been altered without misleading) is the positioning of two leaves on either side of the flower with their midribs suggesting a strong horizontal line, even though the mid-section of this line is missing under the flower. This

50 Pencil line: dog rose, *Rosa canina*

kind of effect, termed *subjective* or *implied* line, may be of great value in a composition, or, as can be seen in this illustration, a distinct minus. If the left-hand leaf were moved so that the tip stood slightly below its present position, the subjective line would be broken and the drawing much improved.

The second weakness was caused by impatience. I did not allow the plant enough time to settle before it was drawn, and after the specimen was completed several other blooms opened to expose their petal forms altogether more agreeably.

HATCHING The use of hatched lines for tone predates the invention of the graphite pencil; the technique was used by artists working in silver-point. Hatching can give an aesthetically pleasing unity; but its almost invariable use until recent times seems at least partly due to the fact that continuous tone (see below) had to wait until papers were manufactured with flaw-free surfaces. With hatched line a few catches or lumps in the paper are not seen.

The hatched leaf in fig. 51 shows that the shading is made up of individual small strokes. Even though the darkest shadows appear solid, the effect is built up with single strokes all sloping the same way. The diagonal along which to shade will depend on whether you are left- or right-handed. The drawings of Leonardo da Vinci have strokes that run from top left to bottom right, the characteristic of a left-hander.

Though consistency in the direction of hatching seems best, this should not be so rigid as to give a mechanical feeling – a look at the works of master draftsmen will confirm that though hatched lines more often than not run in the direction comfortable for the artist, there will be some shifting in angle and often it can be seen where the paper has been moved around. This is especially necessary where the hatching, if consistent throughout, would become clumsily parallel to the enclosing lines of a stem or other feature.

The method used in drawing fig. 51 was as follows: three measurements were made – the total length and the widths of the widest parts on each side of the midrib. The last two dimensions were the same in this case, though often they may differ; even in leaves with one part considerably smaller than the other this is not always as clear as might be expected, venation and serration may confuse the eye. The next step was to put in a generalized outline, taking care to position the widest parts of the leaf on each side of the mid-vein correctly in relation to the base and the apex. In this leaf the widest dimensions are opposite, and a line drawn from one to the other would be at right-angles to the midrib. This is commonly not so (fig. 16a); a line running through the widest portions will not be at right-angles to the centre vein, and the leaf will have an oblique appearance.

After completing the lightly pencilled outline, plus the midrib, the main veins were added – those on the left of the leaf, looking towards the apex, were established first, and were guides for those on the right. Notice whether veins are opposite, or alternate as in this leaf. You will see that though the venation forms an almost regular pattern of more or less parallel curves, there are small variations. At one point two veins diverge from the axis much closer together than the others, and the minor veins are not entirely regular especially towards the margins. Yet overall the impression is one of consistency.

The most stretching task was to draw the serrations; this mode is described as *double-serration*, as most of the main teeth bear smaller ones on their flanks. Each serration is the end-point of a vein, and it was necessary to adjust the lightly sketched vein ends to accommodate each with a tooth.

After the main veins, the more obvious of the minor ones were put in. As the leaf surface at this phase was divided into segments by the larger veins, it was only a question of reproducing the pattern within each area. Next, the first layer of hatched shading was drawn to indicate the broad structure of light and shade, moving from the apex of the leaf to the base.

To make a hatched stroke, place the pencil point firmly upon the appropriate spot – here, along the shadowed side of a vein – and with a flicking motion of the forearm, pivoting from the elbow, make a mark while at the same time lifting the lead from the surface. The marks will be wedge-shaped with the bases describing deeper shadow tapering away towards the apices and the light. After the first run over a drawing the

51 Leaf in pencil hatching

result may be disappointing – much as with the line drawing of the rose at the penultimate stage. A final application of more hatching to the areas of deepest shadow, using very short strokes and continuing until the darkest portions are as close to black as an HB pencil can reach, will add contrast and provide the missing vibrancy and range.

a

b

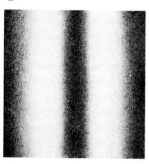

c

CONTINUOUS TONE Areas of continuous tone are made without using separate strokes. The pencil lead is applied with an elliptical motion, moving from dark areas to light and back until the required densities are achieved. As with the previous style, the most satisfactory method of working is to go over the whole drawing establishing broad areas of light and shade, and then to move to and fro over the surface adding emphasis until a full tonal range is represented. There is a freedom and flexibility about this approach which is enjoyable, yet it is entirely suited to studies demanding the greatest discipline and skill. At its worst the use of continuous tone will help the inept, since superficially pleasing results are not hard to produce. And at its best the technique will test the adept.

When applying continuous tone the movement should originate at the shoulder. This seems odd, but as the motion becomes sub-conscious you will find it relaxed and not tiring; when the same results are attempted by moving the fingers alone, the hand tends to clench more and more tightly until muscular tension affects much of the body.

The entire foundation of the technique is seen in the simple gradation exercise in fig. 52a: once you are proficient in moving smoothly from black to white, exciting results may be created. Figs. 53–56 (and the frontispiece) show this basic principle in practice.

You will find that in moving from dark to light, over and back again and again, revolving the lead slightly as suggested earlier, a stage will be reached where the darkest area will not absorb more graphite even though it remains a mid-grey. This is because both surfaces in contact – the lead on the pencil and that already on the paper – become so polished that insufficient friction remains to continue the process. Freshening the lead with the craft knife will provide enough new rough surface to give a much deeper tone to the wanting area. Sometimes it is appropriate to give an area an all-over coat of grey, either to be left as it stands, or to be darkened or lightened later. To keep the grey completely even in tone it is worth exploiting this tendency of the lead to become polished with use: holding the pencil at a shallow angle to the paper (20–30 degrees) and revolving it as you proceed, work over a small area on the protective paper under your hand until the tip has stopped depositing on the graphite-loaded surface. The shallow angle and the turning motion will ensure that most of the exposed lead is polished. (To hold the shaft at this slope, with the fingers well back from the point, you will need a long lead.) The polished lead can then be applied to the area to be shaded, holding the pencil at the same shallow angle and using gentle pressure, but for this type of even, featureless toning the tip should *not* be turned but should be held in the same position throughout. An elliptical movement of the tip will give the most even results: each ellipse should be shallow and about 5mm from side to side. The movement should be continuous, without the lead leaving the

d

52 Continuous tone:
a, b, c basic technique;
d application

paper until the area to be shaded is complete. An ellipse is preferable to a circle, which tends to leave small unshaded areas that have to be filled; horizontal or vertical strokes are not used as they leave discernible lines.

53 Continuous tone, pencil: lichen, *Stereocaulon* sp. (much enlarged)

Restrain the impulse to blend the tones by rubbing with a finger-tip, as this produces a subtle change in quality to a bland and greasy slickness. If too much tone has been added, the solution is to apply the slightest touch of the eraser, but be sure to use an unsullied part or the flaw will be worsened.

Much of fig. 53 was worked over initially in the above fashion. The drawing is based upon a lichen, *Stereocaulon* sp., and for once carries no

54 Continuous tone,
pencil: *Ascarina lucida*

OPPOSITE
55 Continuous tone,
pencil: forest interior, New
Zealand (1)

guarantee of accuracy. My original drawing, at five times life-size, was
only 58 mm (2¼ in.) high, and was rather poorly reproduced as an inset at
that scale; the present study was loosely reconstructed from the published
version for this demonstration.

The method of work was first to make a light outline drawing. Then a
mid-grey was added, covering the whole illustration except those portions
that were to remain white. Finally the drawing was brought to life by the
slow evolution of the shadowed areas through to the deepest parts among
the 'columns' and under the 'altars'. Though the mid-grey was put in by
the method outlined above, it would be misleading to suggest that an
entirely even tone was attempted except in a few areas. In this instance it

was appropriate to vary the pressure on the lead to capture the subtle variations in tone from off-white to around the middle range. The darkest tones were left until the end. Up to that point a continual process of adjustment and balance was made – a darker tone here was balanced by another there and so on until all the options were used up.

For the darkest tones the pencil should be lifted from the shallow angle used for the light areas and held at an acute angle to allow full pressure on

56 Continuous tone, pencil: forest interior, New Zealand (2)

the point. If this is kept sharp the deepest tones will be easier to realize and crisp edges can be maintained.

With experience, you will be able to plan a series of steps towards the completion of a drawing, though the effect of each, as it qualifies earlier work, may also modify steps that follow. Results rarely match completely those anticipated, and continual re-appraisal is needed.

WHITE LINE For fig. 53 the process was one of addition from the beginning, making little use of the eraser other than on the initial outline and to lift off excess tone. In figs 55 and 56 the eraser was used as a drawing instrument to create white line. Until the manufacture of plastic erasers the technique of cutting out fine white lines from a dark area could not be practised with precision and, as it may be unfamiliar, I will describe it here in full.

A plastic eraser of uniform texture, as described on pp. 66-7, lessens the likelihood of crumbling or of the uneven cutting out of tone. The edge should be cut to a sharp chisel form (fig. 57a) with the craft knife (if much of this work is intended, make sure you have a good stock of erasers as the process is fairly wasteful). A few experimental exercises should be tried before using the method on a drawing. Establish an even area of tone with the pencil, then apply the edge of the eraser with a firm even pressure in a series of lines and curves as shown in fig. 57b. You will find that the width of the eraser will not permit a really tight arc so convoluted shapes cannot be followed; also, the edge will rapidly fail, leaving a blurred trace, and this means constant trimming. In spite of these limitations, the results can be well worth while. In fig. 55 the grass-like clumps of epiphytes towards the bottom right could not have been drawn in such detail without this technique. This is also true for fig. 56 where the mosses and ferns, especially those along the base of the plate, could not have been taken out of the dark areas of tone. The delicate white veins on the kidney-shaped ferns were also done in this way. The technique was applied on and off throughout the two forest illustrations.

Fig. 57 shows the evolution of a white-line drawing. To start, an area of mid-grey has several white lines cut out by the eraser. Some of these are blurred in parts, especially where tight curves have been attempted – despite the eraser having been turned to follow the line. In *c*, an extra layer of tone has been added while firming up the edges of the lines. Lastly, the white lines become leaves by the addition of midribs and shadows. It is perfectly feasible to put in or take out leaves during the final stages – the epiphytes in fig. 55, for instance, were established layer after layer. In using this white-line method together with continuous tone very fine detail is possible.

A white pigment could be used for white lines – but there are at least two major objections to doing so: first, any pigment would be over-visible and so would destroy the unity of the drawing; and second, the picture surface would be ruined for further development, since the handling quality of pencil over paint is quite different from that of pencil over paper.

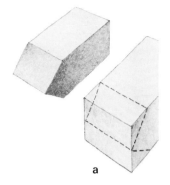
a

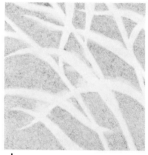
b

c

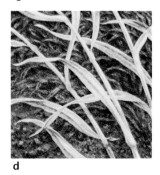
d

57 White-line drawing:
a eraser trimmed for use;
b mid-grey tone with white lines taken out; **c** addition of another layer of tone;
d addition of details

7 Ink

OPPOSITE
58 Stella Ross-Craig
(1906-   ) *Ranunculus bulbosus* L. In *Drawings of British Plants* Vol I, Bell & Hyman, London, plate 31

Ink is nowadays the medium most commonly used to illustrate professional or 'serious' botanical publications. Photolithography will reproduce the most detailed pen drawings, but letterpress line blocks may be less satisfactory; so if your work is to be printed, try to find out in advance what process is to be used, and, if necessary restrict the use of minute detail.

Reduction of ink drawings generally should not exceed one half linear (that is, a quarter of the original image area). I prefer to aim at reproduction at two-thirds of the original length and width – a reduction of one-third linear. If an ink drawing is over-reduced, lines disappear, tonal effects achieved by stippling etc. tend to clog into black splodges in the darker parts and in the lighter areas to burn out altogether. A continuous-tone pencil drawing or a painting will be less affected by reduction than drawings in ink: large paintings, for example, have often been enormously reduced for reproduction as postage stamp designs.

From the above, the use of ink for botanical illustration might well be queried. But the technique is so firmly entrenched in the scientific press that is it hard to imagine its displacement unless information sharing changes radically. In some quarters this position has become a tradition of some rigidity – line drawings are used because line drawings have always been used. However, some botanical journals accept works in other media – including colour when the higher costs are justified. The second reason why ink is used so extensively for scientific illustration is that for the most part it is peculiarly suitable. It is possible to hover somewhere between the realistic and the diagrammatic, and this facility is frequently ideal. In working from living models one may move towards realism (though not as convincingly as with pencil or paint), moulding and texture may be indicated by the addition of tone in stipple or hatching, yet this may be done discreetly so that relevant forms are not obscured. In drawing from dried herbarium specimens it is a distinct advantage to move a step further from realism to concentrate on pure line, or line with the addition of very little tone, in order to avoid misleadingly implying qualities that have vanished with the death of the plants.

Equipment

PENS I would suggest that you try out several kinds of pen – preferences tend to be idiosyncratic and many automatic-type pens are on the market. As for the now old-fashioned nib, my long-term choice has been the Gillott number 290 (in the United States the type is known as a 'crow quill').

There is a certain human quality to the old-style pen, stemming as it does from the quill used over many centuries. There is also a feeling of

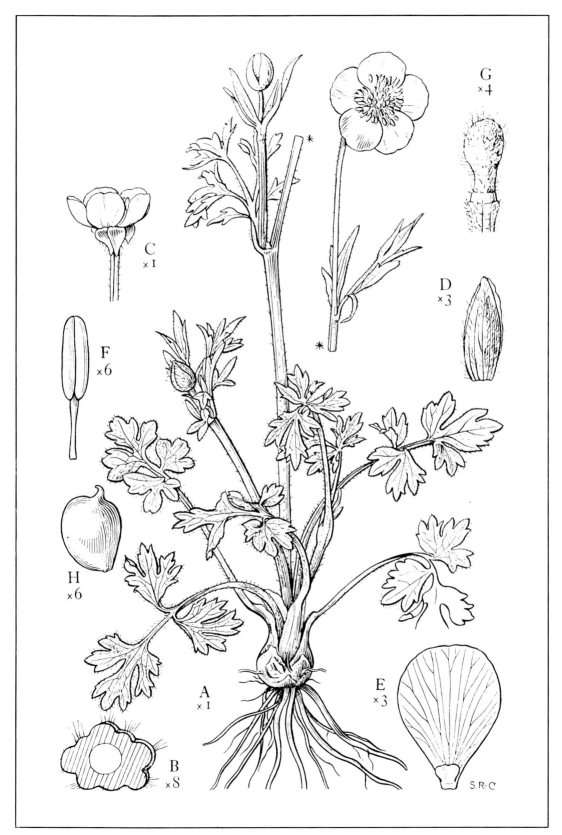

C
×1

F
×6

H
×6

A
×1

B
×8

G
×4

D
×3

E
×3

S.R·C

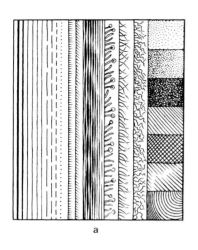

a

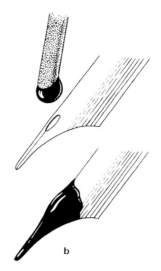

b

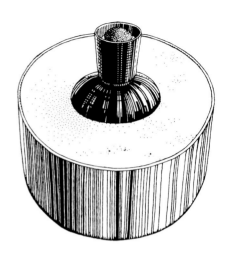

ABOVE AND CENTRE
59 Variety of marks made
by the pen, and method of
loading a nib

RIGHT
60 Stabilized ink bottle

virtue in having conquered a difficult technique: and one is reluctant to let this go in turning to an easier way of achieving an almost identical effect. Objectively, the steel-nibbed pen's continued use for botanical illustration cannot sensibly be defended; all that it can do is more readily managed with the most recent generation of fibre-tipped pens with spirit-based permanent ink which are in a category far removed from that of the earlier felt-tipped models.

A fibre-tip pen of this kind was used to draw many of the illustrations in this book. The pen is a throw-away model, which seems wasteful, but it has a surprisingly long life-span. As shown in fig 59, line-width can be varied as needed by increasing or easing pressure, and by lifting the tip gradually lines can be trailed off. With many earlier re-loadable automatic pens it was difficult to achieve this effect as lines ended in a truncated fashion when the pen was raised. Owing to the protrusion of the fibre-tip, the barrel may be held at an angle as one would a pencil, in contrast to earlier automatic pens which function best only when held close to the vertical. The ink in disposable fibre-tip pens is entirely satisfactory, provided that they are labelled 'permanent'.

For those who would still like to use a nibbed pen, a few hints can be given. The nib should be loaded by pipette (or brush) on the upper side only as shown in fig. 59, in preference to dipping into the bottle, and dried ink should not be allowed to build up on the blades. To prevent this, frequent wiping with a cloth is advised, giving extra attention to the line where the two blades of the nib meet – dried ink in this fissure gradually force the points apart, causing a thickening of the line and a loss of quality.

The past ten years or so have seen a vast improvement in the qualities of drawing inks. Black ink should be truly black and should dry waterproof with a semi-matt finish – all brands that I have used recently satisfy these criteria. The ink sold for use in re-loadable automatic pens is sometimes a fraction less opaque than it should be and this should be watched for. Some inks for nibbed pens have a built-in pipette in the bottle cap, a great convenience for loading.

When using a pen with a nib, the ink bottle should be positioned near enough to allow frequent loading to be done without stretching, but it should be below the level of the drawing surface and out of range of swinging elbows. For those who have a tendency towards clumsiness I recommend the device shown in fig. 60: a greased ink bottle is placed in a shallow container to which you then add plaster of Paris; when the plaster is dry the bottle will slide free to permit easy replacement. This simple tactic renders major spills unlikely.

PAPER As for pencil work, paper should be made of rag. Several rag papers and boards are available with surfaces designed for the use of ink. Some artists like to work on plastic drafting film; this permits easy erasure but otherwise seems to me to be unsympathetic, feeling cold and artificial. 'Board' is the term applied to paper of a certain thickness – as in 'Strathmore' board. There are also various types of 'illustration board' available, consisting of a paper mounted upon a heavy card backing. Boards are expensive (though pleasant to use), and many will prefer to use lighter weight papers which may have the added advantage of being translucent enough to allow one to trace off material where required.

Generally, boards and papers offer at least two kinds of surface, abraded and smooth. The former gives a slight 'tooth' or drag to the pen and the latter allows the nib to skim easily. The difference is subtle and you should give a fair trial to both before deciding which you prefer.

Whatever paper you choose, it should have a hard finish that will not allow an ink line to bleed (spirit based inks are particularly demanding in this respect). A good quality line is fully black with clean margins and no holes. Fig. 61 shows, in magnification, the kind of line to aim for (top); the second line is the result produced by a soft fibrous absorbent surface; and the third is the kind of line yielded by a hard over-textured finish.

61 Ink lines (magnified) on different surfaces

Paper composition should be sufficiently homogeneous and non-fibrous to allow erasure without much 'furring'. Plastic drafting film is perfect in this respect: areas can be removed with a sharp blade, and the surface can then be renewed to *almost* the original condition by gentle use of an abrasive eraser. 'Strathmore'-type boards will permit a certain amount of erasure without much destruction of the surface layer, although whenever an eraser has been used to remove an ink line an attempt should be made to repair any damage by burnishing with a clean pebble or like material. This will help, though line quality will suffer over an erased area to some degree no matter what corrective action is taken. Lighter-weight papers may allow little erasure; it may be preferable to complete a preliminary outline separately and to transfer this to another sheet for the final work. This course may be used as routine where much erasure is needed and where a light-table is available, or where paper is translucent enough to permit a direct tracing.

As with pencil drawing, the colour of the paper is probably most agreeable in light cream or ivory rather than brilliant white.

ERASERS For removing preliminary pencil drawing after inking, the resilient plastic eraser recommended in the last chapter is ideal, but to take out ink a more robust type is needed; it should be very finely abrasive but without scratching or scoring. Abrasive erasers are usually coloured, and in some kinds pigment may be ground into the paper when rubbing is prolonged.

A good hard eraser should last for years: I have a pink one of which about a third remains after use on and off for more than a decade. The main reason for long life is that removal of ink is a time-consuming chore which perhaps makes one doubly wary of making errors. Yet some mistakes are inevitable and it is as well to know how to make corrections effectively.

For erasing ink, a fairly gentle even pressure should be applied in an elliptical or circular movement covering a few centimetres with each sweep. The process will at first appear ineffective, but after a while lines will thin and eventually break before dissolving away. If initially too much weight is placed on the eraser, loosened ink particles may be pounded into the paper; though as lines fade more pressure can be safely applied. With patience, all traces of ink may be taken out: particles should be cleared with a feather, then, as mentioned earlier, the worked-over surface should be burnished with a pebble or similar object, taking care to avoid touching the remaining inked areas.

Paint can be used to cover errors, but for me this is not acceptable as the painted area is always obtrusive and lines which pass over it will change in quality. Though an ink drawing is more often than not intended mainly to be seen as a reproduction, and in this form corrective paint will not be visible, the original will be spoiled. It is a question of pride in the integrity of the work; a sloppy production will give little pleasure to creator or recipient.

Another technique – cutting away – may be used almost without leaving a mark for *tiny* flaws such as hairs that are a fraction too long, or small wavers and blemishes on otherwise good lines. A sharp scalpel should be used to pierce only the top layer of paper around the fragment to be taken, then a corner may be teased up in order to roll the piece away as shown in fig. 62. On no account should these small areas be burnished as ink will crumble from the adjacent cut edges and will be ground into the paper.

Ink

PENCILS The surfaces used for ink are often more resistant than those used specifically for pencil drawing, and where this is so, harder grades of lead are appropriate: 3H to 6H pencils perform well applied with light contact. Soft pencils lose their points too quickly on such surfaces and smear when erased. The hard pencil used properly leaves a faint line which erases easily. A natural error is to use more and more pressure in establishing a correct line, when a complex shape gives difficulty, until the paper starts to furrow. Erase gently before anything like this stage is reached. On the completed ink drawing there should be no trace of preliminary pencil work.

Techniques

Ink, like pencil, may be used for pure line, or in a combination of line and tone. However, there is one major difference between the two media: black ink can make only black marks, and tonal effects are made by hatching and stippling – whereas pencil can be made to range from the faintest grey to almost black by increasing pressure on the lead.

LINE As shown in fig. 61, ink lines will vary on different kinds of paper surface. But necessary as it is to find a suitable paper or board, your most important aim should be to develop the capacity and skill to produce an ascetic precision in line. This is not simply a discipline but also a source of keen pleasure. Once limitations are appreciated, refining and evolving the process may last a lifetime. Pure line is less commonly used than a combination of line and tone; even when working from herbarium specimens it will be found that a *sparing* addition of stipple or hatching will enhance and clarify.

A careful outline is first put in lightly with a hard pencil. Some artists prefer to use only the merest guide lines – a single skeletal line for the stem etc; but by making a precise preliminary drawing with correct measurements before adding ink, you will be able to concentrate entirely upon the inked line.

To ink in a long pencil line with perfect accuracy is demanding. The pencil guide, being drawn with a fine point, should have no width in practical terms, but the ink line does have a discernible thickness and this influences its placement. The eye judges the distance between the inside margins of parallel inked lines (as in stems etc.) rather than from their middles or outer edges, so inking should follow the outsides of pencil lines. How closely this ideal is approached will depend on your ability, especially over a lengthy line.

A worthwhile practice exercise is to draw lightly pencilled curves in parallels and then to attempt to follow them accurately in ink. The use of

63 Ink line drawing of rosebud reproduced at two-thirds and half original size

parallel curves is sensible, as much time is spent on stems, petioles, peduncles and other structures of this character. A drawing of a long linear leaf, stem etc. should appear to have been drawn with unerring strokes in a relaxed hand. This is the impression to strive for, though in truth I have never had the fortune to possess such skill or even to meet it in others. Unhappily, work done with broad gestures, though sometimes pleasing to the eye, cannot satisfy the stringent requirements of botanical reportage. Precisely inked lines, especially when of some length, are usually made in a number of movements, lifting the pen from the surface as each terminates, and gradually replacing it as the next span is started. You may find it necessary to change position or to move the paper as the sequence progresses. Each section should be completed in a fairly slow, even flowing motion and the pen should be lifted smoothly without flicking as the tip leaves the surface. The pen is re-applied just prior to where the last section begins to tail off. Joins between segments when done with skill are undetectable. As noted earlier, when drawing and inking parallel lines, the left-handed will find that the right line is best done first to serve as a guide for the one on the left, and the right-handed will be served best by the opposite approach.

A relaxed attitude is vital to the creation of good work. It is not easily cultivated or maintained, and a constant guard must be kept against the intrusion of tenseness. Muscle tension often originates in the fingers and can be avoided by remembering to work from the shoulder or elbow.

An ink line drawing may not necessarily be enhanced by tone – which should always be employed with a particular artistic or botanical aim, and not used simply to fill blank spaces. Also, when drawings are going to be much reduced in reproduction, an uncluttered work will, if boldly done, stand up to the process better than one hatched or stippled. As with pencil, it is surprising how much information can be conveyed by line alone. The small rosebud in fig. 63 shows how pure line may record essential form and how this kind of line will reduce. The sketch is shown here at two-thirds and at half the original size. Appropriate reduction helps to minimize irregularities and gives a general improvement in appearance.

TONE Few ink studies are done in pure line; more often tone is used to add information. Fig. 64 shows how a tonal effect in ink is based upon dots (stipple) and lines (hatching). Areas of tone are shown magnified so that differences in technique are apparent. Viewed with half-closed eyes, the result is broadly the same throughout; but in close-up the stipple as in *a* and *b* gives a quite different appearance from the hatching of *c* and *d*. The last two leaves look somewhat coarse and casual in contrast to the pair on the left. With stippling a far greater control is retained and fine detail may be shown.

Most botanical artists appear to settle into being either stipplers or hatchers. In my own case I started as a hatcher and became a stippler as frustration pushed me into a technique better suited to recording minute detail. A rational approach is to skip from one mode to the other depending upon the requirements of the moment – where simple bold drawings are needed use hatched tone, and reserve the use of stipple for subtle modelling.

Time may also be a factor – to complete a delicately modelled form, a stippled drawing may take twice as long as a hatched version, though it may also be twice as satisfactory.

To work faster in stipple without sacrificing quality I often use a modification as in *b*. Moving from light to dark I start by using dots quickly replaced by minute strokes which gradually move closer together until they fuse into black. A rhythmic movement is established which does not seem to work for pure dots; transitions from grey to black are accomplished more smoothly and reproduction seems marginally improved. Small dots remain preferable for use on structures such as petals which require a very light touch.

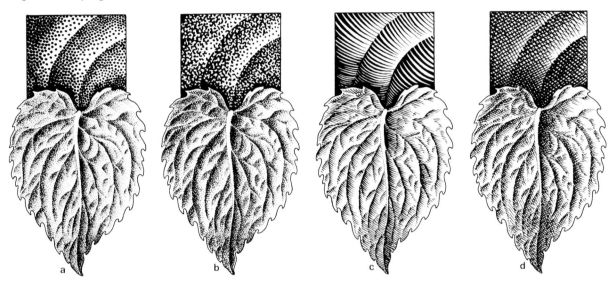

64 Shading: **a** stipple; **b** modified stipple; **c** lines following leaf surface contours; **d** lines following leaf surface contours plus hatching

The illustration of *Epilobium latifolium* (fig. 65) indicates further how tone may be used in ink. The layout of the insets, the use of instant transfer type and the grouping of the scales (see also p. 145) may also be of interest. In this plate, drawn with a Gillott 290 nib, a method of showing the shaded sides of stems etc. is illustrated; this may be thought pernickety, yet especially where narrow parallel lines are concerned it is not easy to gain the same effect in any other way. A detail is shown in fig. 66a¹. This type of shading is faster to do than it might appear; a press and flick movement is used and all stems and branches can be covered in minutes to add finesse.

Take care not to allow the drawing to become too dark. This can be avoided if tone is used to reveal form, not simply to fill space. With experience an over-dark plate will not occur. If an illustration as a whole has become too dark it may even be appropriate to repeat the work, as correction of large areas is a lengthy process with often not entirely satisfactory results. Small portions may be erased as described on p. 000, but areas exceeding a few centimetres in diameter should be blotted out with acrylic or other waterproof paint (bearing in mind reservations expressed earlier). For the finished appearance of the drawing it is as well to attempt to match the paper colour. The painted area will not have the same agreeable working surface as the untouched paper and even if great

	mm	
a,a¹,b,c,c¹	10	
b¹,e	5	
b²	1	
c²	1	
d	0.5	

skill is used the repair will be to some extent visible – at least to the artist. To avoid getting into this position, beginners should err on the cautious side and make their work rather too light to start with, as this condition can easily be corrected by an extra layer of tone.

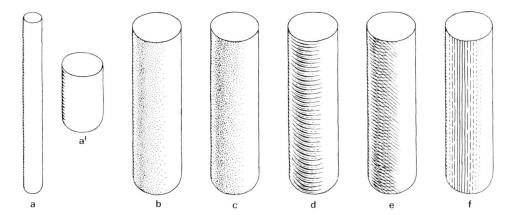

a a¹ b c d e f

Dissections

Flower dissections are usually portrayed in ink. A high degree of accuracy is required and it may be necessary to use more measurements than are usual for whole plant or habit studies. Here scale becomes of prime importance. Sometimes, with larger flowers, it will be sensible to work at life-size, examining detail with a hand-lens; dimensions may be transferred directly, using dividers or a ruler. More often than not flowers will be too small to handle in this way and then a dissecting microscope is used. Generally, as in fig 65, there will be an area of the plate set aside for the dissection: this governs the scale used. It is helpful to have an even magnification where this is to be mentioned in the text (but see p. 145) – in other words ×2, ×5, ×10 etc., rather than an enlargement by, say 2.65. If a bar scale is to be used, and if you have a pocket calculator, an uneven magnification is no problem; on the contrary, it may be of advantage – especially when fitting the flower snugly into an allocated space. With the memory function of the calculator, each dimension – derived by reading from the micrometer eyepiece scale of the microscope – can be multiplied in the blink of an eye. Further hints on working with magnification are given below as drawing a flower dissection is described step by step.

To start, a discussion usually takes place between artist and author as to what should be shown and what should be emphasized. Emphasis does not imply exaggeration, rather clarification; for example, pollen clumps might obscure a stigma and the shape should be revealed by their removal; or perhaps hairs about the bases of the stamens migh be seen only by moving the light source; again, a minute feature such as the shape of the connective tissue between the pollen sacs might be of special interest. Sometimes it may be necessary to take out particular characters to be placed in separate detail studies.

In selecting a flower, a number of specimens should be looked over before deciding what is typical. It is not rational to aim for an absolute in

66 Stem shading: **a** 'flick-shaded' side of stem as described in text; **a¹** enlargement of **a** to show detail; **b** stipple; **c** modified stipple; **d** lines following stem contour; **e** lines following stem contour plus hatching; **f** vertical parallel lines

OPPOSITE
65 Ink study: *Epilobium latifolium*. a × 1, habit; a¹ × 1, capsule; b × 1, flower; b¹ × 3, stigma/style; b² × 5, ovary apex; c × 1, upper stem leaf; c¹ × 1, lower stem leaf; c² × 20, leaf detail; d × 40, seed; e × 3, axils

this respect, you can only reflect what is true in a specific place and time. Nevertheless, through consultation and perhaps prior reading you should know of special circumstances. For example, a species might be *monoecious* – where anthers and carpels are borne on separate flowers on the same plant; or there may be a developmental sequence with changing relative proportions of the sexual parts.

A decision will also have to be made as to how much of the flower tissues are to be excised in order to reveal essentials. In a single study the organs removed can be noted in a caption, though in a series this information may be conveyed once in the text rather than by constant reiteration. In the hypothetical flower of fig. 67, three stamens and one petal have been taken.

It is a natural assumption that the flower should first be taken from the plant. As noted earlier, flowers often collapse rapidly after major surgery; this is more true of blooms removed completely from the plant body, the process of deterioration is slowed if the operation can be managed on the flower *in situ*. This solution occurred to me after several years of petals etc. browning and distorting almost too fast at times for adequate recording. The technique can be used only where it is feasible to manoeuvre the flower, still on its stem, under the microscope; for this the plant must be growing in a pot and must be flexible. Any opportunity of working in this way should be taken, as drawing may then be at a more considered pace.

If the flower has to be taken from the plant its useful life may be extended by placing it on a bed of moist cotton-wool or blotting-paper in a petri dish or similar shallow container. The cut surface of the flower stem should not be exposed to the air but tucked away in the 'bed'. With flowers that break down quickly, it is helpful to draw as much as is practicable before dissection. In a specimen such as that in fig. 67 all the exterior portions may be completed in pencil before exposing the interior.

Despite all precautions, some flowers will not stay usable long enough for completion. When this happens, make a note of all dimensions before going on to finish from other specimens of the same stock. It is more acceptable to do this than to add in measurements from a second bloom, as, though shapes and structures should be the same, even slight differences in flower size will result in distortion. Almost always it should be possible to finish the pencil drawing – a second specimen may then be used for reference and checking while inking in.

Once the flower has been selected and is in place, drawing should proceed as rapidly as is compatible with accuracy. It is sometimes worth making a quick preparatory sketch. This might be done when you lack experience and wish to note all the parts to be measured in an orderly way before starting, or if the flower is extremely complex and an analysis will help in determining procedure; or it may be that an irregular scale, as mentioned above, is to be used, and it will be found time-saving to calculate all conversions in one operation. Such a rough working sketch, need bear little resemblance to the finished study – it is enough to show the parts that are to appear. In fig. 67a, the initial sketch has been made before full dissection has taken place. Here, the front petal and the upper

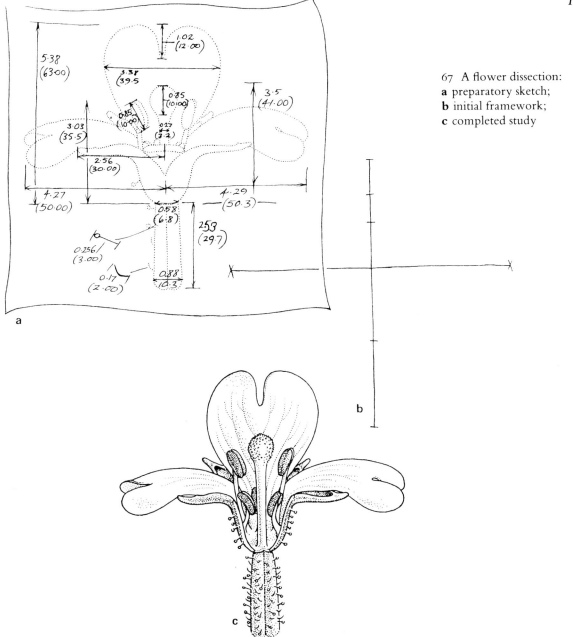

67 A flower dissection:
a preparatory sketch;
b initial framework;
c completed study

parts of two stamens have been trimmed back (using small scissors) without cutting into the calyx or floral tube. Flowers often tolerate this amount of interference without visible response. Comparison with the final version shows the few further measurements that have to be taken after full dissection.

For measurements to be read without confusion, the rough sketch is done in pencil, the figures are entered in ink, and the conversions are in ink of another colour. This sounds fussy but it is simply a matter of having a couple of pens of differing ink colours to hand.

In fig. 67*a*, the upper figures are in millimetres as read directly from the micrometer eyepiece scale (see p. 23). It has been assumed for this demonstration (reduced by one-third linear) that a space of *c.* 105 mm wide was left on the original for the flower dissection, and so each dimension has been multiplied by a factor of 11.7 in order to fit the drawing in comfortably. The upper figures are arbitrary in this example and bear no necessary relation to any real plant.

In the finished study, fig. 67*c*, a number of fairly subtle details have been shown clearly. Features will differ from species to species, but several items here indicate the kind of detail to watch for. These include: the depth of notching on the petals; the shape of the stigma and the extent to which the stigmatic papillae descend the style; the points from which the stamen filaments arise and the way in which the anthers join the filaments; the distinctive moulding of the apices of the calyx lobes; the types of hairs and their distribution; the faint pattern of venation on the petals; the cross-section shape of the ovary as suggested by the line at the base; and so on. You may notice that the rear petal is in an unnatural position in relation to the others: this posture accurately reveals the shape of the petal which otherwise would have been hidden by foreshortening. When flowers lie flat under the microscope, it is usually easy to move a rear petal to show its shape. Where this is not feasible, it may be desirable to remove and detail one separately.

Notice also that the hairs on the calyx and some of those on the ovary are glandular as shown by the secretions at their tips. This is the kind of feature that disappears from dried material.

In fig. 67*b*, the initial steps in establishing the flower are shown. It was assumed that a certain width was available with a less critical limit to the height of the flower, so the horizontal axis was entered first. A measure was then established from the extreme left to the vertical axis: the dimension runs from the left petal-tip to the line which runs conveniently through the ovary, calyx lobes, style and stigma, and the notch in the rear petal. In an actual flower it would be unusual for all these points to line up quite so neatly. However, in flowers of this type the columnar style provides an obvious key line, and generally this will at least be aligned with the ovary as in this instance. With the vertical axis in place, procedure became straightforward. Care was taken to place the dimension from the apex of the ovary to the tip of the rear petal in a pleasing position in relation to the rest of the plate, as this measure fixes the flower. Next the stigma, what was seen of the style, and the notch at the petal apex were entered. These were followed by the rear petal width; then attention was turned to the anthers and all parts visible of the upper and lower sets were drawn. (As noted elsewhere, anthers have the disconcerting habit of dehiscing on exposure to the warm dry air of the studio, though this process may be slowed where the flower is backed by a moist pad.) After adding the lateral petals, the calyx lobes and other external features, the floral tube was cleanly sliced to remove the petal stub, two remaining cut-back stamen filaments and one complete small stamen. From dissecting several flowers before the final selection, you will know just what will be revealed when the interior is exposed; often, as in the present example, this is simply a question of drawing in the base of the style together with the points from

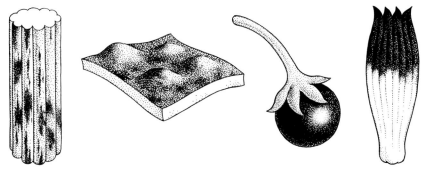

which the stamen filaments originate. Nectaries may be seen, or perhaps hairs will be arranged in a particular pattern, etc. Sometimes it is necessary to use a brush to clear the base of the floral tube of nectar.

It would be more usual to draw a complete ovary, though here I have followed a practice used in an extended series illustrating the genus *Epilobium* where it was considered that little would be gained by showing the whole ovary in each species.

As mentioned above, by the time a dissection has been drawn in pencil, the flower itself may be wilted and a similar bloom may be used to refer to while inking in. When the lines have been inked, stipple is used, with extreme restraint, to reveal and clarify detail. In fig. 67c, stipple helps in defining such features as the anthers; the concave areas of the calyx lobes; and the ovary - note especially the way in which the sinus runs down the centre. Venation is also shown by extra-light stippled lines on the petals.

A useful tactic is shown in the way in which hairs break through the line of the ovary. The hairs look more convincing if they are inked first so that the line describing the edge of the ovary may be broken to leave minute gaps where they emerge or cross; this is related to the convention of breaking lines where structures cross one over the other - used by some in a rather affected form. Breaks in the line should be used only to avoid ambiguity - and even then they should not be obtrusively large.

As noted above, the anthers in fig. 67c are differentiated from surrounding tissues by the addition of stipple. Had they been in fact of the same tone as the background there would still have been sufficient reason for treating them in this way, though probably less stipple would have been used. This raises a problem. It is almost axiomatic that one should not try to represent colour and colour changes in black ink. Yet there are times when it is more misleading if an attempt is not made. Perhaps a petal will carry strong markings, or the stems of one species may contrast with others by being dark. The one criterion to apply is that of ambiguity - if tone is applied in a particular area, could it be taken to represent shadow indicating moulding of the surface? And, just as important, if tone is used to show pigmentation in one sector, this must not lead to doubt about other parts where its use is intended to interpret structure.

In fig. 68 this concept is put to the test; forms are treated as if they are strongly pigmented. There is no problem about recognizing where tone represents colouring except in the leaf section (second from the left) where one cannot be sure where shadows end and pigment begins: a situation where it would be wise to confine attention to structure.

8 Scraper board

Scraper board (scratchboard in the United States) allows a drawing to be made in white by removing portions of a black ink film with an engraving tool to expose a white underlayer.

Advantages are that a highly dramatic effect may be achieved with some ease; white detail may be placed against a dark ground; gradual modulations of tone from white to a true black are possible without difficulty; extremely fine lines may be drawn; and corrections are not tedious. Scraper board is flexible: I have used it for anatomical studies appearing in scientific journals, plant illustrations for interpretative works such as plant guides for National Parks etc., and also for cover designs.

There are drawbacks. The technique is time-consuming, and, when used for illustration, the text may easily be swamped unless care is taken to maintain a pleasing balance of black and white. One has constantly to blow away black powdery detritus as each mark is made – though this is a minor irritation, and the action becomes automatic. A small technical snag with ready-primed (black) scraper board is that the main design is best drawn separately before transferral by tracing. Also, scraper board use may become over-facile, a quality seen sometimes in advertising examples.

Notes in chapter 7 about printing ink drawings apply equally well to scraper board.

Equipment

SCRAPER BOARD is comprised of a card faced with a white china-clay preparation. Upon this a fine layer of black ink is added by the manufacturer or the artist. The ready-primed blacked board is used when most of the surface is to be worked over and few large areas of solid white are to remain. White board is preferred where considerable areas are to be left white: black ink is then added to the appropriate sections as required.

Though scraper board appears quite thick and robust it is in fact brittle. Bending should be avoided and edges treated gently as they chip; corners are especially vulnerable. Board is available in a wide variety of sizes. Unless large-scale works are definitely planned, it is better to buy small to middle-sized sheets.

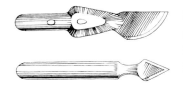

69 Scraper tools

SCRAPER TOOLS (fig. 69) may be bought, though many artists find that they evolve and make instruments to suit their own styles. Whatever your eventual preference, cutting points and edges must be kept extremely sharp by the frequent use of a fine-grained stone.

MISCELLANEOUS ITEMS Apart from a whet-stone, little else is needed other than an HB pencil for direct drawing, or red-crayoned paper for transferring designs from preliminary drawings to the board. Though the commercial red-transfer paper is useful, a satisfactory substitute can be made by rubbing pencil lead over a sheet of thin paper. HB to 2H pencils are best, as anything much harder does not transfer clearly, and softer grades spread surplus graphite around too freely. A fine sable brush is useful for adding ink to white scraper board.

Techniques

Before doing a finished plant portrait in scraper board, a certain amount of preliminary doodling and sketching will help you to gain control over the tools and to appreciate the variety of marks, lines and textures that are easily made. Fig. 70 shows this kind of exercise on both black and white board. Rather different effects are obtainable from each style of board so at this stage they are discussed separately.

In starting with the ready-primed black board it will be found that parallel lines may be incised with almost mechanical precision. This facility allows the use of parallel hatching for indicating light areas in a manner similar to the way in which pencil and pen hatching is used to show shadow; though for finest detail a modified stipple is better.

Although, as illustrated, the effect changes with each doodle, the line is in fact the only basic component: even the apparent dots are minute wedge-shaped lines (in contrast with true round dots possible in pen stipple). Marks made with a vertical up and down motion will be almost invisible; to make anything approaching a dot stipple, the scraper tool is applied to the surface in a flicking motion. The resulting tiny wedges are useful in imitating many plant surfaces. These small flicks tend to run in one direction: random movement is not easily accomplished on scraper

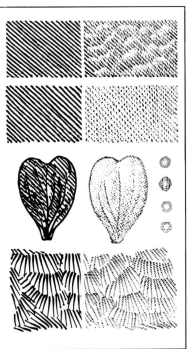

70 'Doodles' on ready-primed (black) and user-primed (white) scraper board

a

b

board as the tip of the instrument digs in or catches when direction changes are attempted.

White, unprimed scraper board may be treated in exactly the same way as ready-primed board if Indian ink is first brushed on in an even, thin layer and allowed to dry thoroughly.

An advantage of white board is that it allows one to use the method shown in fig. 70*b*. The doodles here were first made in Indian ink with a pen or fine brush (as shown on left) before being worked over with the scraper tool: some untouched portions are included for comparison. This demonstrates, as noted above, that white board is especially useful where large white areas are to remain.

The pencil for preliminary drawing should be an HB or similar medium grade as harder leads will damage the surface. Even with an HB, pressure should be light; erasures can be made in the normal fashion with the type of eraser recommended for pencil. Pen lines will be wider than when working on ordinary paper – the extra smooth surface of scraper board allows the ink to spread very slightly. This is disconcerting initially, though the extra width gives more scope for the scraper tool.

For some topics on white board it is sensible to make an ink drawing much as described in chapter 7, excepting that tone will be more freely used to exploit the properties of scraper board. Stipple or hatching can be added in the usual way and built up until the drawing overall is darker than the usual pen-and-ink botanical illustration. Be careful to build the ink up evenly, otherwise the cutting tool will incise clearly in those areas where the ink is applied thinly but will leave rough edges where application has been over-lavish. Experiment will show just how much ink is too much.

When using unprimed board, I prefer to apply ink with a brush to an area just exceeding that of the projected design outline; the area required is decided by tracing off an approximation as shown in the inset in fig. 71. Two coats applied thinly are usually sufficient to give an opaque and even covering, with the first layer being touch-dry before the second is added. The plant drawing is then transferred to the prepared ground in either of two ways. If the initial drawing has been made solely as a step towards a scraper board study, and if it is on thin paper, it can be placed over the inked area, with red-crayon or leaded paper interposed, and traced over with a well-pointed hard pencil. The original should be firmly held in place by tape. For an original containing extremely fine detail, the hard pencil is best replaced by a dissecting needle, pricker, or similar sharp point. This may cut through the drawing in places but the resulting line will have greater clarity. Each line described by the sharp point should be placed exactly where required as it will be lightly engraved into the ink and will only be removed by the scraper tool; for most originals the use of a hard pencil is a better practice as a pencil trace may be removed by gentle use of the eraser.

The second method of transferring the design should be used where the original drawing is not to be damaged. This may happen quite often, as for instance when work completed in another medium also has potential for scraper board. If the original is to remain untouched, fix tracing paper over the top and trace off a copy using the lightest practicable pressure; then continue as described above. This preliminary tracing can be omitted if you have access to a photo-copier, as the copies are thin enough to be used for the first method.

71 Leaf study, *Rubus*, on user-primed (white) scraper board; (inset) excision of leaf margin from outline

With the design transferred, cutting can begin – but check first that the ink is completely dry: even a slightly damp surface will result in an ugly mess rather than a crisp line. Experience will indicate how long ink takes to dry under different conditions. A test can be made in an area to be trimmed away, and if this is satisfactory, the unwanted ink areas extending just beyond the design boundaries may be removed.

In doodling you will have noticed that tool *points* incise thin lines that increase in width as more pressure is used, and *edges* take out areas. Consequently a sharp *edge* is best used to trim away outside the design. Tools will only perform effectively on scraper board as long as they are

72 Scraper board: *Bignonia* hybrid

kept really sharp. As the design is revealed, start blowing, as mentioned earlier, with the lips puckered to form a funnel, and continue until cutting is completed. A continuous air-stream should be directed at or about the point of the instrument – an undirected occasional puff is not enough. Even a small area of ink will yield a surprising amount of debris which quickly obscures the work if blowing is not kept up.

In releasing the design from its surrounds, the sweeping cuts made to take out the unwanted areas should be kept shallow and smooth. This is an insurance in case it is later decided to extend the original concept – not easy to do if deep scratches are present.

If you have difficulty in following a finely traced-off line, use a raking light shining almost horizontally across the board. The pencil line will then shine as if inscribed in silver. Going over the pencil line with the very tip of a pointed tool will render it still visible when the side light is removed.

Once the extraneous surround is cut away, work may commence on the exposed plant silhouette. The sequence should be from medium light to dark – that is, areas catching the light are engraved first with the 'flick-stipple' or hatching tailing away into the dark, but no attempt is made at this phase to show bright highlights or wholly white areas. These should be saved for the final touch when the drawing will spring to life as the brightest portions are shown. This does not mean that lighter parts should be left completely black until the last stages; on the contrary, the overall tonal structure is best established early, followed by a gradual working towards the lightest state at the end.

With pencil and pen caution has to be used to avoid work becoming over-dark – but with scraper board you should try to avoid any part becoming lighter than intended; hence the strategy of *slowly* strengthening all the lighter areas until the finish. If an area becomes lighter than intended, more ink may be added – but reworking is never as satisfactory.

Fig. 72 shows a completed scraper board study done on ready-primed black board. This was used as a cover design. Note the way in which different texturing is used for various parts of the plant body.

There is a similarity in appearance between wood engravings and some scraper board drawings. The former medium is sometimes consciously imitated, but most would agree that scraper board is best exploited for its own strengths.

9 Water-colour and gouache

Water-colour has been the medium preferred for plant portrayal over many centuries. Pliny the Elder mentions the names of several who painted herbs, including Krateuas whose work was copied and recopied: his paintings were used to illustrate Dioscorides' *De Materia Medica* of the first century AD. Probably the earliest versions were unillustrated but it was not long before the paintings of Krateuas were incorporated. None of his original work survives, though something of its quality may be gauged from copies in one of the better-known versions of Dioscorides' manuscript, the *Codex Vindobonensis* made for Juliana Anicia, daughter of Flavius Anicius Olybrius, Emperor of the West in the year AD 472. This dates from about AD 512 and the water-colour illustrations, even though they were imitations, remained a high-water mark for almost a thousand years. They were probably done using the opaque water-colour known as body-colour or gouache, rather than the transparent style now preferred by many.

Despite the discovery that oil could successfully be used as a binding agent for pigments, botanical artists have in the main continued to work in water-colour. Oil paints have never been serious contenders except for works such as the Flemish and Dutch flower-pieces. There are a few painters of botanical subjects in oils today, whose work indicates that the medium is not unsuitable, but it is still true that most prefer to use the simpler, more direct medium of water-colour.

Most of the pigments in artists' quality water-colours are transparent. The advantage of this is that coats of different colours may be applied, each qualifying its successor in much the same way as would occur in layering stained glass, and the white of the background paper shows through to give highlights or a translucent glow. Painting in this vein is often termed 'pure' water-colour.

In contrast, gouache or body-colour (the terms are synonymous) is opaque water-colour which may be obtained by mixing a little white pigment into transparent colours, or can be purchased ready for use as gouache, designers' colours or poster colours. Its opacity makes gouache much easier to use than transparent water-colour – mistakes are obliterated by an extra coat or so, and an area may be worked over several times. Lighter tone may be placed over dark with confidence, which also allows gouache to be used on toned or tinted paper. In spite of these properties, there are also losses to consider. These are not easily defined, as they are not absolute but matters of degree. Without transparency there is a little less brilliance (though this difference is lessened in reproduction) and sometimes a slight chalkiness and an altogether heavier quality than in 'pure' water-colour. For some the disadvantages are unimportant compared with added flexibility; others find the drawbacks important but use opaque colour here and there; and there are purists (myself included) who generally spurn opacity except to show white hairs, venation and similar details that cannot be completed by other means. You will discover with experience which approach suits you best, but it does seem that the term 'water-colour' should be reserved for work that is in the main transparent.

In discussing opacity versus transparency it should be mentioned that where a subject demands something of each quality – for instance, light stems painted over a deeper background, with the whole modified by transparent washes or glazes – then thought might be given to working in acrylics (chapter 10).

From this point 'water-colour' refers to the transparent form. Gouache is discussed on pp. 124-6.

Equipment

WATER-COLOUR PAINTS come in two forms: tubes or pans. People seem to have strong preferences. My own choice is definitely for pans, though this may be a minority view. Pan colours are immediately available as required – one can survey the ranks and move from pan to pan swiftly, pausing only to wash and squeeze out the brush to avoid contamination. A marred pan can be cleaned with a stroke of a wet brush. It is sometimes argued that pans of paint can become tough and hard when not in constant use, but this is true only of poor quality paints. Whether you choose pans or tubes, make sure that you buy 'artist's quality' water-colours.

Once you have decided which of the several excellent brands to use, thought should be given as to which colours should be included. This question is largely decided for you when buying a paint-box set, as each company prepares ranges – from 'beginners' outfits to truly opulent selections. If water-colour pigments included a pure cyan blue, a primary yellow and a good transparent magenta, it would be possible to mix virtually any colour from these – just as the printer does with his inks (though for demanding works the printer adds grey and sometimes other colours). However, all pigments fall short: it seems axiomatic that, in searching for a primary hue, if the colour is more or less as required then its handling qualities will be inferior – it will not be transparent or it will not be entirely compatible with other colours in mixing, so several different blues, yellows and approximations of magenta are required. This last hue gives the greatest problems to the botanical artist – so many flowers have petal colours from this part of the spectrum, yet it seems impossible to find pigments to depict them accurately without tolerating deficiencies in the paint itself.

Foxglove and thyme are two common flowers that nicely illustrate the difficulty. Each species has blooms that are near magenta with a touch of blue – the hue referred to as rose-purple in botanical literature. Cobalt violet, with a hint of carmine or alizarin, will reflect this handsome colour but it contains about the worst handling features of any pigment. It is muddily opaque and does not mix well with other hues. There are occasions when nothing else will do – but its use is kept to the very minimum, and from time to time I try new colours in the hope of finding a replacement with a better character.

To some degree all pigments have faults: these may be clear on first use, or they may emerge slowly. Probably it is best to start off with a nucleus of good quality colours, and to add to these over the years to solve particular problems. A capacious container will allow for supplementary purchases.

In the following list of essential colours for the botanical artist some, such as the cobalt violet noted above, violet lake and the earths are more often used in minute amounts to modify other colours. White is there to make body-colour for hairs etc. Black is excluded because an excellent black may be mixed in the palette. As detailed on p. 116, reds, blues and yellows in correct proportions make a black somehow darker than the manufactured ivory or lamp black, and this same mixture in dilution gives a wide range of greys – varying from warm to cool to neutral depending upon the relative amounts of each ingredient.

Recommended hues are: 1 lemon yellow; 2 cadmium yellow; 3 vermilion; 4 alizarin crimson; 5 *carmine; 6 cobalt violet; 7 *violet lake; 8 cobalt blue; 9 French ultramarine; 10 Prussian blue; 11 viridian; 12 *sap green; 13 burnt sienna; 14 Chinese white. These should cover most needs though the enthusiast will certainly be driven to try more. Asterisked colours are rated as being only moderately durable and they should not be used in works intended to provide a permanent record.

Experience in using each colour will give an understanding of its physical properties. Each differs in some respect, usually slight, from its fellows. For example, pigment grain sizes are not always constant from one colour to the other, and this factor explains why, in colour washes derived from an equal mixture of two components, one often dominates on drying. Again, some colours are not absorbed by paper to the same extent as others and tend to lift when an attempt is made to add another layer.

There are too many variables to attempt to catalogue the peculiarities of all pigments used individually and in combination – each maker's pigments sold under the same colour names differ slightly; responses to various papers may not be the same; colours in combination may behave differently from when they are used singly, and so on. The only advice that one can responsibly give about the handling qualities of water-colours, is to try them all out singly and in mixtures in the kinds of exercises suggested below.

BRUSHES are no less important in the production of a fine plant portrait than are high quality colours. There are many choices including several synthetic fibres as well as traditional ox-ear, squirrel, sable and others.

The qualities to watch for when purchasing brushes are their capacity for holding liquid and retaining their shape, and – especially important for the botanical artist – that when wet they come to a good point without any tendency to split. Suppliers allow the prospective buyer to wet brushes in order to check this feature and often provide a water-container for this purpose.

For brushes, as for paints, it is not hard to suggest an essential few, and they too will grow in number, though for a different reason. Most top quality brushes are close to perfection, until they start to wear; and then all but the steel-willed buy replacements without throwing out the old.

The first decision is what type of brush to buy. There are round-tipped and flat-tipped, both with either long or short handles. The choice for botanical work has to be for round tips and short shafts; a round tip is best suited for most organic subjects and a short shaft is more comfortable for working at close-quarters. There is little to separate reputable makes carried by artists' suppliers, but hair type offers several options. The best brushes, without doubt, are sable. These are expensive, but if the cost is weighed against useful life, probably the dearest are in the end the cheapest per mile of paint. Have at least the smaller grades in sable. I have tried several 0–1 grade synthetic fibre brushes, because of the difference in price between these and sable, but they proved unsatisfactory – the final half millimetre or so was too flexible and would not hold a consistent point for long. I have not used the larger sizes in synthetics – these may well be suitable for washes and broader treatment. At the time of writing, brushes of mixed synthetic fibre and sable have been introduced and these seem promising. Ox-ear and squirrel hair are also best kept for less detailed work.

You will manage perfectly well for most botanical topics with four sizes. Two of grade 0 are needed because one should be reserved for use with white paint for hairs etc. – white paint seems to wear a brush more rapidly than other pigments. This is also a function into which a grade 0 brush may be retired as it starts to lose a few hairs, as one fined down in this way may be perfect for handling delicate white detail. Grades 1, 3 and either 8, 9 or 10 make up the other essentials. The brush most in use is grade 3, though for mixing large amounts of wash I use grade 8 or 10, and for minute subjects 0 and 1 are ideal.

Brushes are precision tools and should be properly cared for. Pigment must not be allowed to dry on the hairs, especially where they enter the ferrule. If paint is allowed to accumulate in this area, it forces the hairs apart. Even after a spoiled brush has been thoroughly cleaned it may refuse to point well.

If brushes are to be stored for a long period it is as well to put them into an air-tight tube with a moth-ball. And whether brushes are stored or in daily use, points should not touch the sides of the container or anything else for that matter; contact gives a tip a bias or breaks it up, and restoration takes some time.

PAPER A sensible tactic is to try as many rag-based papers as you can, noting the good and the bad features of each. A final choice should not be made too swiftly, as some features are not necessarily appreciated at first.

Many papers can be discarded at a glance, others may have to be put aside on the grounds of expense – some French papers for example are far too costly for most day-to-day work. Paper with a rough grain or texture should be avoided for botanical illustration as this may show in reproduction and it makes detail more difficult to capture. A slight 'tooth' is helpful in holding pigment – entirely smooth hot-pressed paper is not satisfactory. An eventual choice may well be between a surface that is minutely too rough and one that is fractionally too smooth. Weight is also of some importance in that the heavier grades, 140 lb (*c.* 63 kg) weight and above do no have to be stretched (weight refers to a ream). This small advantage is offset by the greater cost of heavier types and the fact that the process of stretching paper (see below) renders it more responsive. Lighter weight paper must be stretched to prevent cockling or buckling which otherwise is inevitable when washes are laid down. Illustration board – fairly light paper, ready mounted on cardboard and so pre-stretched – is also available, though again expensive.

PALETTES   The depressions on the lid of the paint-box are usually quite sufficient to hold pigment and water mixtures for washes etc. but there are times when these will not be enough. There are ample palette forms to suit personal tastes, and there is probably little to choose between them for effectiveness. My preference is for a porcelain variety that may be stacked and so kept dust-free.

WATER-JAR   The perfect water-container is glass, squat, capacious and with a fairly narrow mouth. Glass allows the state of the water to be monitored: when painting dark areas muddiness can be tolerated, but light and subtle topics such as flower petals require clean water. Squatness signifies stability – a tall container may look elegant but will beg to be tipped over. Capacity should be large to minimize the number of water changes. A fairly narrow opening lessens the scope for spillage, but it should be wide enough to allow the brush entry while your attention remains partly on the model or the painting: for some operations in water-colour it is imperative to move swiftly, with the action of washing out the brush being semi-automatic. It is a help to keep the jar in the one position. The brush may then be placed blindly; with a smallish opening, entry is confirmed by the first wiggle clicking on each side.

GUMMED BROWN PAPER STRIP   Used in stretching paper, as described below; it should be no narrower than 5 cm (2 in.) or the stretching paper may pull free.

LIGHT-WEIGHT DRAWING-BOARD   A light-weight board placed upon the regular drawing-board gives so much extra flexibility that it is hard to imagine working without it. Water-colour paper stretched on to a light board may then be picked up, turned around, and worked on from any direction. The angle of the working surface may be changed by adjusting the regular board underneath or by tilting the light board by hand. This supplementary board may be of any stable material that will not stain the paper – 5 mm ($\frac{3}{16}$ in.) thick plywood or hardboard (masonite in the US) is ideal, cut to about 50 × 40 cm (20 × 16 in.). For small subjects a piece about 40 × 30 cm (16 × 12 in.) will provide even more ease of movement. If necessary you can work solely on the light board without a regular drawing-board or drawing-stand underneath provided that some means is devised for tilting the light board to various angles. When painting on heavy illustration board a light-weight board is superfluous.

MISCELLANEOUS ITEMS Absorbent rag or paper towelling is used for taking excess water from the brush each time it is washed. The material should be lint-free and should be hung between your lap and the drawing-board on whichever side is most convenient. This, like the water-jar, is often used automatically without looking. For the rest only a plastic eraser, pencils HB, H, 2H, and a feather for brushing away eraser particles are needed.

Techniques

Volumes appear yearly on painting in water-colour, but the methods of realistic plant portraiture are to some extent the reverse of those advised for landscape and the like. For the latter style of painting one works broadly in washes, and fine detail is thought of as niggling and not to be indulged in. Botanical art demands a disciplined precision giving maximum information; yet the aim is still to avoid an over-laboured effect by using simplicity and economy in each phase.

Before working on a plant, try the exercises below as a means of getting to know about the behaviour of each pigment and the ways in which different papers respond. Some papers will not need stretching for this preliminary work as, for the most part, each area worked on will be too small to make cockling a problem. However, it seems sensible to explain the stretching method first.

STRETCHING This is best done near a bath or sink to speed the sequence. Although the instructions may seem lengthy and complex, the operation will take only about a minute from wetting the paper if you are deft. Before starting, lay out what is needed on a cleared table-top or bench. Cut the paper to fit with ample margins on the light-weight board placed close by; cut gummed brown paper strips to allow an overlap around the sheet (fig. 73), and put a tea-towel or small hand-towel to one side. The sink should have enough water in it to cover the paper.

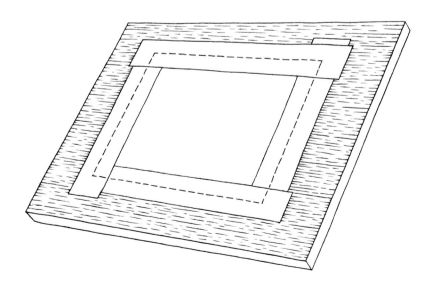

73 Stretched paper on drawing-board

1 Submerge the paper. Some recommend that it should remain under water for three or four minutes, but I have always found that thirty seconds or less gives complete wetting; in fact, some papers are slightly damaged by longer immersion.

2 Place the sheet on the drawing-board, holding it by two corners (top or side – not diagonal) and allowing the bottom edge to contact the board first, to be pulled into position as the rest of the sheet is laid down.

3 With the paper in place, cover it with a towel to absorb surplus water – dabbing so that the two materials are touching more or less throughout. Rubbing or horizontal movement will harm the paper surface. The smallest delay will allow the paper to start cockling. Sometimes this step is omitted but removal of the excess water ensures adhesion of the gummed tape.

4 Apply the gummed paper strips in turn, holding them at each end by finger and thumb and passing them through the water in one motion, and then placing them in position while held taut to present a non-sagging surface. Each strip should have about half its width on the drawing-board and half on the paper.

5 Finally, touch the gummed tape gently with the towel to remove free water, using minimal pressure to avoid squeezing gum over the paper.

Stretching paper should be left lying flat so that drying will be even over the entire surface. A tilted board may allow water to seep towards the bottom giving an uneven drying rate – uneven pressures over the paper may then cause it to tear or to pull free. Accelerating drying by the use of a heater or direct sunlight may have the same result.

The paper should be left to dry for some hours. The length of time varies depending upon room temperature and humidity. It is rash to work on an incompletely dry surface as preliminary pencil drawing leaves score marks, erasure is impossible, and paint will be absorbed too freely, blurring out over margins. As a rule I make a practice of being if anything over-careful with drying, usually stretching paper at the end of one day to use on the next. The paper must remain under tension until the painting is completed; then it may be cut free with a scalpel or craft-knife. The way the paper then pulls aside from the blade shows how much tension is involved in the process.

From the time the paper is placed wet on the board to when the completed painting is cut free, take care not to rest your hands on the area to be painted over. Grime, perspiration and body-oils do not mix well with water-colour. At some stage everyone discovers the irritation of putting down what is intended to be an even wash only to have it broken by speckles of grease. A protective sheet of paper under the hand (recommended earlier for use with pencil and pen) is equally helpful here for trying out colour mixes and brush strokes; to see how a particular wash mixture will dry; and to see how one colour will behave when laid over another and so on.

OPPOSITE
Gerard van Spaëndonck (1746-1822) *Campsis radicans* (L.) Seem

OVERLEAF LEFT
Pierre-Joseph Redouté (1759-1840) *Paeonia suffruticosa* Andrews from *Description des plantes rares cultivées a Malmaison et a Navarre* by A. J. A. Bonpland, Paris, 1813

OVERLEAF RIGHT
Franz Andreas Bauer (1758-1840) *Strelitzia reginae* Banks from *Strelitzia depicta*, London, 1818

Pæonia Moutan Mr. b.

To avoid having to replace this practice-cum-protective sheet frequently, take a piece about A4 size and fold it in half. When the half under the hand is filled up, open the sheet and fold back in the opposite direction for further use. When this exposed area is full, the sheet may be folded again to give a quarter of the original area. At no time should a doodled surface come into contact with the working area.

WASH Before painting a plant it is essential to acquire several simple techniques. One is that of putting down an even wash of colour; this is basic to water-colour painting and is easy on almost any paper that is not over-smooth.

The first step is to draw ten or so rectangles – 8 × 5 cm (3 × 2 in.) is a useful size. The definite boundaries help to teach control of the brush. Label the painted results – 'one layer', 'two layers', 'wet on wet', 'wet on semi-dry' etc. – to provide a reference (fig. 74).

The drawing-board should be sloped at an angle of about thirty degrees to allow the wash to keep moving down under the brush, without being steep enough to permit an uncontrollable run.

Mix a wash of any hue well diluted with water in a paint-box reservoir or palette. The amount of colour used is not critical but it is best to use light tones until the behaviour of the paint and the paper are assessed. Mix more wash than you are likely to need – this is a good habit to acquire, to avoid running out when only part way through an area.

A grade 3 brush is used for small sections such as these – though when you have mastered the technique you might also test it on bigger areas using the largest brush. The 8 × 5 cm rectangles will allow many possibilities to be presented on one sheet. The technique (fig. 75) for laying in a wash is:

1 Load the brush in the wash mix. The hairs should absorb enough to swell the tip without risking drips (*a*).

2 Apply the brush to the top corner of a rectangle and take it in one stroke to the opposite corner, holding it at a shallow angle so that the line of pigment left behind is broad – part of the body of the brush is used rather than the tip alone (*b*). Paint will accumulate along the bottom of the stroke – if this threatens to break and dribble the drawing-board is at too steep an angle.

3 When the first stroke is completed, make a second stroke a fraction lower down to return to the side started from (*c*). If the first stroke yielded ample pigment along its lower edge the second movement may be continued without lifting the brush from the paper. However, if the paint has not formed this reservoir, the brush should be reloaded. Depending partly upon the absorbency of the paper, it will probably be necessary to reload for the third sweep across.

4 Follow this simple process until the bottom of the rectangle is reached – back and forth strokes with a well-loaded brush. Keep enough pigment on the brush to give an accumulation at the bottom of each stroke –

OPPOSITE
Ferdinand Lucas Bauer
(1760–1826) *Flindersia australis* R. Br.

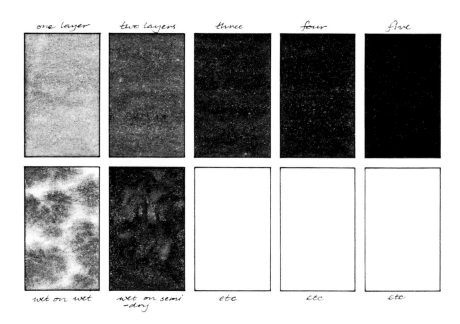

one layer   two layers   three   four   five

wet on wet   wet on semi-dry   etc   etc   etc

74 Layout for wash exercise

though this can be allowed to lessen as the bottom of the rectangle is reached. Ideally the last stroke will finish off so that a slight twirl of the brush-tip will lift all surplus wash as the last corner is reached. Often this does not happen and a runnel may remain at the base. If this is left, the bottom edge will dry darker and perhaps more unevenly than the rest. The remedy is to wash the brush and squeeze it semi-dry on the rag, then take the brush-tip along the accumulation, absorbing it throughout. If a surplus still remains the brush should be washed, squeezed out again, and the action repeated.

Depending upon the quality of the paper, the dilution of the pigment, and your skill, this first rectangle may dry with an even finish as intended, or it may be streaky. A streaky result may be improved on in the next try if the area is painted over initially with a wash of clear water. This is especially helpful if the paper has not been stretched, though even stretched paper can be made more cooperative in this way.

Apply the wash technique to most of the ruled-up panels, keeping a few in reserve for further experiments suggested below. After the first coat has

75 Wash technique

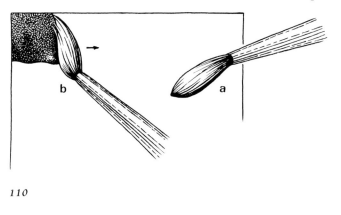

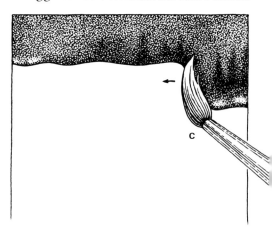

dried thoroughly, try a second layer. One panel should be left with only one coat so that a difference may be seen between this and the rest. Continue to exclude one panel with successive layers so that one rectangle has one coat, the next carries two, the next three and so on, up to five or even six layers of wash as in fig. 74. Depending upon the variables noted earlier, at some point the paper will absorb no more pigment, and no matter how patiently you wait for the wash to dry, an attempt to add another coat will only dislodge earlier layers, with unsightly results. It becomes second nature to be aware that this stage is near and to hold back.

The remaining rectangles are worth using to find out what happens if you cannot wait for a wash to dry before trying to add to it. An attempt to add when the wash is over half dry is usually a mistake – instead of adding pigment the brush picks it up. You will quickly learn that an even wash (as in the underlying colour of a leaf) is best put on speedily and then left until dry. This is not to say that one pigment may never be introduced into another on *wet* paper – one to several colours may be mixed and modified in this way *provided that the surface remains wet.*

GRADATED WASH When you have practised putting down an even wash, another necessary basic skill should be attempted – a gradated wash. Though in water-colour it is axiomatic that one works from light to dark (light colours cannot be put over dark without using gouache or other media), with this technique you can start with a pigment which may be at maximum density or any degree of dilution needed, and then by adding water in steps work through a tonal gradation to a predetermined lighter tone or to clean paper (fig. 76*a*). The technique allows you to move in one coat from dark to light on a leaf or stem etc. Generally such gradations on plants are found over short distances – a petal dark at the outer edge fading to white at the base would be typical – but the ability to establish such a change over larger areas is also worth cultivating. The method is not complicated but the achievement of a perfect gradation is elusive.

a

Draw a series of columns approximately 8 × 3 cm (3 × 1 in.) on a sheet, stretched or not depending upon how your papers performed when an even wash was put on. You may or may not wish to pre-moisten the area within each column before pigment is added, again depending on previous results. Then proceed as follows:

1 Load the brush as before.

2 Apply the brush as with the wash technique except that when you reach the point where you wish the tone to lighten, dip the brush-tip momentarily into water instead of the wash mixture. This will dilute the pigment already on the brush and on the lower edge of the previous stroke as the next stroke is taken across.

3 Depending upon the degree of gradation aimed for, more water may be added with each alternate stroke or with successive strokes, until the base of the column is reached.

b

76 Tonal gradation

It is possible to speed or slow the transition by adding or withholding water. The most rapid gradation is made by washing the brush after the first stroke, wiping it gently on the rag to take some of the water, and then taking the brush-tip across the lower edge of the paint to absorb and lift off pigment. It may be necessary to wash out the brush once more to add another stroke in water before mopping up surplus in the same way as with the even wash technique.

A second or third coat may be needed to reach the depth of tone aimed at in the darkest section of the column, remembering that the underlying coat must be dry.

For some papers, it helps to add the water-diluted pigment, and later the pure water, *not* to precisely the lower edge of the last stroke, but to a point 3–5 mm (*c.* $\frac{1}{8}$ in.) above. Then complete the stroke in the usual fashion, remembering to use part of the flat of the brush rather than just the tip. All brush movements should be made with a feather touch.

In trying out the technique it is useful to mimic a stem (fig. 76*b*). Turn a column to a horizontal position and grade off the wash to about the centre, allowing it to dry before turning it about to do the same thing on the other side. By varying the depth of tone on one side or the other, different lighting effects may be simulated.

In some situations a reverse of the procedure described above may be needed, starting with clear water and adding the wash mixture by degrees until the brush is loaded with this alone.

DRY-BRUSH Another route to colour gradation is to use the dry-brush technique. The term is slightly misleading: 'moist-brush' would be a more accurate description. Dry-brush allows colour modifications, strengthening or shading, to be added in a considered way without the speed required when applying a wash – and it may also be used where a further wash coat would result in damage.

In the description below it is assumed that areas are to be darkened to suggest portions of a leaf surface turning away from the light as in fig. 77. The leaf is shown enlarged so that the technique may be more readily followed. At the stage at which dry-brush work commences, an area would already have been established carrying an even wash broken by venation and highlights. Before starting this exercise, check the way in which these features are produced (pp. 113–14). Then proceed as follows:

1 Dip a grade 3 brush into the wash mixture and drag it over the rim of the reservoir leaving the hairs with only a small amount of liquid, reducing this further by trial strokes on the practice sheet.

2 Then apply the merely moist brush to those wash areas that require strengthening, using short vertical strokes with a light touch. Move from light towards shade, treating in turn areas bordered by veins. If the upper edges of the strokes starting in the lighter sections dry in hard lines contrasting with the underlying wash, the pigment mixture has not been diluted enough. Each stroke should dry to blend in imperceptibly at the top, where less pigment is deposited.

3 Move from one side to the other of each portion treated, while continuing gradually down the sheet. This is much like applying an even wash,

except that short vertical strokes are used instead of long horizontal ones. There should be no hint of pigment running to collect at the bottom of a stroke – if this happens the brush is too wet and it may cause damage: a few more strokes on the practice sheet will solve this problem.

4 After completing all the areas with the extra coat of pigment added by dry-brush, the sequence may be repeated again and again, starting each time a little further into the shadowed part of each piece. A number of layers can be added without the surface breaking up, until the density needed in the darkest parts is achieved, or until the paper will not absorb more.

Though dry-brush allows details to complement broad washes, its over-use gives a laboured quality which is the antithesis of the freshness typical of fine water-colours. Plan the initial washes so that most of the work is completed before dry-brush is used for finishing touches. An exception to this stricture is inevitable when minute plants are portrayed – when there may not be room to manoeuvre washes. Dry-brush was also used as described for the ivy leaf on p. 120–21.

77 Dry-brush shading

WHITE AREAS In using water-colour it is necessary to plan ahead, seeing the work in stages. One consideration is the areas that are to remain white. If they are fairly large, they may be skirted by a wash, but difficulties arise when small portions are to be left. There are mechanical ways of leaving white areas – wax, rubber solution and other aids are sometimes used – but none has proved satisfactory enough to recommend. I have so far found only three practices worth using (fig. 78): the first (*a*) is the obvious one

a

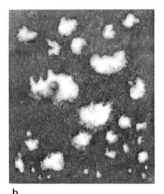

b

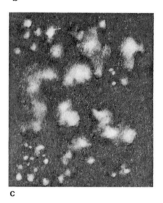

c

78 Effects of three methods of taking out highlights

already noted of painting around the area to be left, allowing the brush just to stray inside the borders; then, if it is possible to pause, the brush is quickly washed out, dried on the rag and used to mop up the excess pigment to create the blurred edge typical of highlights on leaves etc. Speed is essential to ensure that the lower edge of the wash does not dry; the line formed when this happens can't be hidden without adding a further highlight or similar camouflage.

A preferred method (*b*) is to leave small areas, with pigment just inside the boundaries as described above, until the wash is dry. Then, with a clean and slightly moistened brush-tip, the excess pigment can be lifted off at a more comfortable pace by breaking and blurring the hard edges which have been left. The brush should be washed out from time to time to keep the point clean.

The third method (*c*) is best used where a perfectly even surrounding wash is required, or perhaps where there are so many small white spots that it is impractical to paint around them. The wash is taken over the whole area without any attempt to avoid the intended light spots. After the wash has dried, the moist, clean brush-tip is applied to each spot in turn to rub and absorb some of the pigment – which should be washed away in the water-jar. The clean tip can be applied again and again in the same way, until no more pigment lifts off. The process should be stopped well before the paper surface begins to fray. Experiment will show when this point is about to be reached with a particular paper. This method rarely takes out all the colour and so should not be used where clear white highlights are the aim. Small errors may also be erased in this way. For treatment of larger errors see pp. 123-4.

VENATION The venation of leaves may be picked out by an adaptation of the above method. A brush is filled with clean water, squeezed to give a chisel-shaped tip, and drawn along the surface in alignment with the vein. As the sharp tip is drawn back and forth a few times over a short distance – no more than two or three centimetres – pigment is abraded away. The brush should be frequently washed and re-shaped. If the tip is not kept clean, dislodged particles will be deposited along the edges of the vein leaving two dark margins or 'tide-marks'. If the brush-tip is allowed to break from the chisel shape, the cut out line will progressively widen. With a properly shaped-up brush, the lines created may be hair width, and surprisingly few strokes may be needed to indicate fine veins. The effect is illustrated in enlarged detail in fig. 77; it was also used in the plates illustrated in colour on pp. 117 and 118 (bottom).

COLOUR The following exercise will provide a permanent record of the appearance on paper of each of the colours in your paint-box and can be kept to hand as an aid for colour mixing. As the botanical artist is much concerned with accuracy a thorough knowledge of how each colour behaves is invaluable.

It is a help to arrange the colours in your box in the order given on p. 100. At least ensure that all the yellows, reds, blues, greens and earth colours (siennas, umbers etc.) are kept in groups. To avoid confusion, keep the pigments in the same order as they are applied in the exercise. For example, if on your reference sheet you have lemon yellow preceding chrome yellow, and the sequence is reversed in the paint-box, it will be easy to mix one when the other is intended.

Having arranged the colours, rule up on paper enough small panels for all the current pigments and an extra few to allow for later purchases, leaving a space around each for names to be entered (fig. 79). As more hues are acquired they may be integrated into the paint-box sequence; and, if you are methodical enough, painted into the extra panels – with a note indicating their position in the box.

Panels are then filled in with a fairly full-bodied wash from each colour in sequence. Several interesting discoveries are made as the hues are added: most pigments will behave well, drying evenly and with a reasonable density. Some, mixed in the same fashion, will probably turn out darker than expected. Violet lake and Prussian blue have surprising depth of tone, which can be recorded on the chart as a reminder to use them with care. A few pigments are likely to dry in streaks, and are best used cautiously – cobalt violet and alizarin crimson are examples. Sap green also manifests unfortunate tendencies on some papers and should not be trusted – an initial wash may dry with a hint of streaking, and often an attempt to add

79 Water-colour trial layout. Numbers correspond with those in list of colours on p. 100

a second coat will even more severely disturb the first. However, on some papers it is compliant, so it is worth keeping as a rich green not easily matched by mixing.

As a refinement, a second layer can be added to part of each rectangle to show two densities of colour.

The subtleties of colour mixing are best self-taught as it is impossible to give more than a few general hints. Most readers will know that if reds and yellows are mixed the result will be orange; blues with reds yield violets and purples; yellows and blues give greens; and reds and greens produce browns. A fuller treatment of colour mixing is reserved for the chapter on acrylics (pp. 132–4), where results may be less familiar. Apart from some slight differences in effects, the information given is equally applicable to water-colour and beginners in this medium may like to do the mixing detailed there.

Even those with some experience of water-colours may not have come across the mixture for black mentioned on p. 100. Equal parts of vermilion and ultramarine with a very little cadmium yellow will produce a black which at its deepest can be distinguished from the commercial product by a marked lively quality and a darker appearance. Other reds, blues and yellows may be used, though this particular mix is recommended for its stability – with some combinations a second or third coat is prone to lift the underlayers.

Manufactured ivory black and lamp black reflect more light, giving a greying effect; the above mixture appears to absorb light to yield a virtually true black. The dullness of the ready-mixes is evident in comparison. The vermilion–ultramarine–yellow combination also gives excellent shadow colours contrasting with the dead greys of diluted ivory and lamp blacks.

The botanical artist will develop a knowledge of all the various greens that can be coaxed from the paint-box. To try out as many greens as possible (in addition to those purchased) use all the yellow/blue combinations and then look at the results of adding minute amounts of other hues as modifiers; for instance, a lemon yellow/ultramarine mix with a hint of vermilion.

MODIFYING Even after a colour has been tried out on the protective sheet, the result may not be exactly as intended. When, for whatever reason, the hue as laid down is inappropriate, a modifying colour may be applied. For this much depends on how much pigment is already present; as noted earlier some papers reach their saturation point quickly and an attempt to add another layer may fail. Experience is the guide here – though to avoid the worst, one can usually find a tiny leaf, or perhaps an unobtrusive portion of a larger one, to make a test on. The methodical worker may already have a part on the try-out sheet carrying the same number of washes as the actual painting and this may then be used. If the area to be changed is close to saturation, much the same effect can be produced – though more slowly – by dry brush. In any event the practice sheet should be used to find out the exact density of pigment and the hue required to correct the original colour, carrying the modifying colour over the area where the original wash was tried out; only a portion of this

Keith West

should be covered at a time, to allow the difference between treated and untreated sections to be gauged.

Trial runs over practice areas are necessary because various factors combine to make it difficult to pre-assess the likely results. It is hard to see in the mind's eye the *exact* effect of, say, dilute pure vermilion over a green which is already a mixture. Water-colours tend to dry lighter in tone than they are when wet; and different kinds of paper will affect responses – some that are extra-absorbent seem to suck an added colour down into those already present, while others keep the pigment on the surface, sometimes giving a stronger effect than intended.

Occasionally the use of an overlying colour is the only way to reach a particular hue, as some pigments when mixed together in the palette are somehow slightly dulled by the process. For instance there is a purplish-blue that is not uncommon in flowers: in analysing its components you might think that either cobalt blue or ultramarine mixed with carmine should get close to the mark, yet when this is tried the result is somewhat leaden. A carmine wash over the top of the blue yields a colour that is subtly more vibrant.

In getting to know how colours interact, a pleasant and useful exercise is to paint a series of horizontal strips followed by overlying vertical strips as shown in fig. 80. Each colour is used, including the shadow-mix described above. The underlying horizontals should be painted in at about half maximum density, in perhaps two thinnish coats, depending upon the characteristics of the working surface. The overlying vertical strips will be most effective if they are thin enough to allow the under-colours to show through clearly. A little experiment will suggest the right density to use.

FIRST PLANT SUBJECT Your first botanical subject in water-colour should be a simple one such as the ivy leaf on p. 118 – a suitable choice, as the species is available from many localities throughout the year, and it will stay in excellent condition for a long time after picking. Also, it is a model which requires the use of washes – even and gradated; lifting off pigment; blending in edges; colour mixing – including shadows; and the addition of an overlying colour by dry-brush.

A scrap of illustration-board was used for the illustration; on this a drawing in HB pencil was made, detailed enough to show the major veins. Smaller venation was not indicated as it would have been hidden by the first layer of paint. The study then moved through the following stages:

1 The paper was dampened as the hard surface needed to be made more absorbent. Water was applied as for a colour wash, inside the drawn outline, with a grade 3 brush.

2 A wash was mixed of sap green plus a little permanent blue. Sap green performs adequately on this surface – though there might have been a problem had an attempt been made later to carry a modifying wash over the darker areas.

3 After being given a good stir around, the wash mixture was added as described on pp. 109-11, treating separately each section defined by the

Water-colour and gouache

OPPOSITE ABOVE
Water-colour: *Rhododendron campylogynum*

BELOW
Water-colour: ivy leaf

119

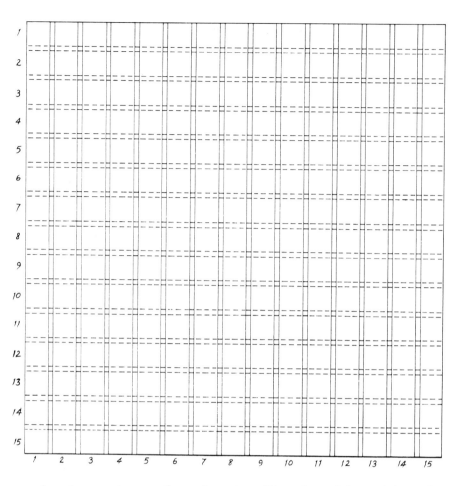

80 Layout for exercise using overlying colours. Numbers correspond with those in list of colours on p. 100, except 15 which may be used for a shadow mix

main veins running out from the point of insertion of the petiole to the centre of each major lobe. Each of these veins provided a line at which the wash could conveniently be halted before moving on to the next section. As each new piece was started a minute gap was left to define the vein in white. The lower lobe contained several much lighter areas and these were described by a steeply gradated wash with more pigment added again towards the tip of the leaf to give a reverse gradation. At the completion of this phase the leaf appeared as segments divided by five white veins in a green wash grading away to white paper in places.

4 Next the minor veins were shown. As mentioned earlier, the aim with tiny veins is to give an accurate impression without following each nerve to its microscopic conclusion. The method used was that described on p. 114, using a flattened moist brush-tip. The edges of the main veins were also softened by the same process.

5 By the time the venation was completed the wash was thoroughly dry, and another layer was added in places using dry-brush, working away from the light areas towards the dark. This second layer reinforced subtly shaded places such as where the leaf surface dipped in slightly on the right of the midrib and the numerous points where veins caused similar changes. When this addition had dried, it was seen that some portions receiving less

light needed yet more pigment – this was dry-brushed delicately without disturbing the two under-coats. The final use of this colour was to add line (with an eroded grade 1 brush) to the right margin here and there where the thickness of the leaf was exposed.

6 While the last touches of green were drying, the petiole (leaf-stalk) was painted with a lightly loaded brush using carmine with small amounts of other hues. A second layer was then added to the left, shaded side of the stalk.

7 The pale yellow-green of the main veins was then put in; the smaller veins were already the correct colour, since incomplete removal of the wash pigment had left them pale green.

8 Next, well diluted permanent blue was dry-brushed sparingly over the lightest areas, bearing in mind that the more thickly coated adjacent greens would easily be lifted. Many artists leave highlights a stark white; to me this should be reserved for the very brightest shiniest surfaces, whereas any area of slight to medium gloss will, in natural conditions, reflect sky colour. An unobtrusive light blue adds realism.

9 For the final work on the leaf, a shadow colour was mixed of vermilion and French ultramarine in roughly equal amounts, with a brush point of yellow to give the mixture a slightly more neutral tint. This again was just drifted over the darker left lobes.

10 The shadow colour was then added as an even wash behind the leaf. This faintly gimmicky touch is inappropriate for most botanical topics, but it was fun to do in an exercise. After the even wash had dried, dry-brush was used to put more depth into the inner parts of the shadowed area; a hint of violet lake was also introduced. The outer edges of the shadows were faded away, using a moist brush-tip with clean water; and in the same way a small highlight was lifted out of the petiole.

SECOND PLANT SUBJECT On completion of the exercise based on a single leaf, you will have gained enough expertise and confidence to carry out a larger study such as that on p. 117. This painting of the common nasturtium *Tropaeolum majus* was thought of primarily as a water-colour exercise for this book and was kept simple for this reason. An example of a water-colour botanical study carrying a great deal more information about a plant is shown on p. 118 (top).

The nasturtium illustration puts into practice in full scale the exercises and information given earlier and tried out on the ivy leaf, so it is necessary only to note a few special features. Firstly, the flowers themselves bring to mind a factor that every botanical artist must recognize: though some petal hues are easily depicted in paint, others are quite impossible to capture with accuracy. It has to be accepted that neither the ingenuity of the manufacturer nor the skill of the artist can match the glowing colour seen in even quite common blooms. Curiously, when a painting is seen apart from its living model this lack is less evident.

A pigment used at full intensity in order to approach the depth of colour of the plant tissue will often appear far too dark in tone on paper – deep, rich colours produced by the interplay of light and living tissue may appear sadly heavy in a painting, even when the actual hue is within the range of the paint-box. The answer is to key your painting (and this applies to any colour medium used) to the brightness of the paper rather than the unrecordable light of the most vivid part of the flower. The tonal range available to the artist, from black to white, is only a portion of the scale in nature which in many flowers extends to brilliance rivalling sunlight. It is therefore often necessary to sacrifice colour intensity, and hence tone, to capture at least the illusion of brightness; though usually it is still possible, while keeping the overall tone of the flower light, to put in some saturated colour in portions that are less fully lit. An adjustment has also to be made in recording shadowed or darker areas: since brilliance beyond a certain fairly low level cannot be matched, it will be seen that unless shadows are reduced in compensation, the painting will be over-dark. Though this concept seems involved, you will realize the problem immediately you tackle a brightly hued bloom. In the nasturtium painting the shadows have been slightly muted – it is not hard to imagine how dull and heavy the flower would appear if the darker tones present in life were fully represented.

It has been argued that the botanical artist should not show shadows other than by a deepening of local colour, because shadow colour may obscure local colour. In practice only the extraordinarily ham-handed would allow this to happen to a point where the hue of any part of a plant would be in doubt. Shadows reveal form and they should be used with intelligence and restraint. Too much reliance upon shadow colour may have a deadening effect, the work will be greyed and the strength of shadow as a tool lost. In subtle hands, however, the application of shadow, usually at the final stages, will bring a work to life. Except on a light surface, and in the darkest portions, the viewer should not be made aware of shadow as a definite colour. On the lower lobes of the two larger nasturtium leaves, shadows have been used in this unobtrusive way – the green was also intensified, but it is the thin layer of shadow colour that gives the impression of undulation.

A final point about shadows is that they are rarely grey falling away into black. Shadow colours vary greatly in their make-up, depending upon factors such as the colour of the sky, surrounding local colours etc. This is especially important to the artist when handling light objects – white to pale coloured flowers are examples. A basic shadow mix (p. 116) may easily be qualified by an admixture of other hues to reflect correctly any particular situation.

Colour changes due to translucency should also be noted, as they convey extra information about the subject. Some leaves, for instance, will entirely block the passage of light, others vary in the extent to which they allow its transmission. Nasturtium leaves are relatively thick but, as may be seen in parts of the large leaf on the right of the illustration, light does pass through to some extent. Where the lobes are turned so that the light pierces them from behind, the quality of the colour changes from being a matt, fairly glaucous green, towards emerald. Provided that this shows in reproduction, those who 'read' the work as it was intended will recognize these areas as translucence. Though ambiguity is normally to be deplored in botanical illustration, there are inevitably some subtleties which only the perceptive will correctly interpret – just as sometimes delving is required to unravel some plant structures.

The translucent effect is achieved by the method used in adding bluish highlights to the ivy leaf. A gradated wash was applied tailing off in the outer lobes, and allowed to dry before the brighter green of translucence was put in with a lightly loaded brush. The whole leaf was then worked over with a darker green to simulate the rucking of the surface by the minor veins.

You may notice that the larger veins stand just proud of the lamina as they approach the centre – minute shadows indicate this feature. Another small item to observe is the red on the margins of the leaves, which also appears in lighter form on other parts. Coloured leaf edges, unless they are unusually prominent, are often missed even though they are present in innumerable often entirely unrelated species.

ERASURE Minute flaws may be taken off using the technique described for the manufacture of highlights, veins and the like, but bigger mistakes should be handled as follows: a large-sized brush should be used if there is space to do so; this is loaded with water which is transferred to the part for correction and left for a few seconds to allow the grains of paint to loosen while the brush is being squeezed into a semi-dry state. The brush-tip is then lightly taken over the area to soak up the freed pigment – initially little or no rubbing is necessary, since a full load of pigment will be lifted. This is washed out and another brush-load of clean water is applied to the correction with a soft rubbing motion. As the paint comes away, the brush is washed before being used to rub again. The sequence may be repeated until the point is reached where damage to the paper surface seems likely. Unfortunately, paper once coated with water-colour cannot be returned to its untouched state. A residue of pigment always remains – and attempts to take out the last vestiges are likely to spoil the paper surface. If the painting is intended primarily for reproduction, the offending portion may be left untouched provided that it can safely be omitted by the printer without leaving an unsightly gap: simply pencil around it with a request to leave out the encircled piece.

You may prefer to preserve the appearance of the finished painting by one of the following gambits. Sometimes, to return the paper to white, the only feasible method is to remove as much pigment as possible without damaging the paper as described above, and then, after drying, to use several thin coats of white tinted slightly to match the paper. This imperfect solution is rarely used in water-colour, partly because anticipating the difficulty of complete erasure leads one to take extra care; and almost always there is an alternative. Usually extra foliage etc. can be used to mask the error, once the bulk of the pigment has been lifted out and the work is completely dry. Occasionally something may have to be taken from what is otherwise an integral part of the painting – as where a section of leaf has to make room for flowers. This kind of correction is rarely completely successful: the removal of pigment cleanly from the edges of an irregular area requires not only patience and skill but also that the material to be inserted is darker than its surrounds in order to hide deficiences underneath. If white or pale features are to be added, the use of gouache will almost certainly be required.

WHITE FLOWERS Portraying white flowers on a background that is itself white is a recurrent problem. On a single plate the best solution is to place the flowers against leaves, where this can be done without distortion; but in a series of white or pale-coloured flowers, this becomes boring by repetition. Another tactic is to shade petals so that they stand out some-what, but if the shadow is too dark it may be mistaken for pigmentation, and if it is too light, petals may disappear on printing. Also, this is disappointing to the eye – white flowers may be spectacular and it seems sad to loose them on the page. A strong outline would look out of place in a water-colour otherwise lacking line. In some situations a tinted ground works well, but coloured backings are better used with gouache or acrylics. Sometimes the area behind light flowers may be lightly shaded or coloured with a blurred outline, as in the shadow thrown by the ivy leaf on p. 118. This can look quite good, though when often repeated it seems contrived and also has an archaic air.

Gouache

There are many botanical subjects for which gouache is a sensible choice: these include plants which have a waxy bloom; those with a covering of densely felted hairs; and species with large white or pastel-hued flowers. Though the terms 'gouache' and 'body-colour' both refer to opaque water-colour, 'gouache' is more commonly used of a painting totally, or in the main, in opaque colour; and 'body-colour' is preferred when only portions of the work are opaque – in these instances phrases such as 'with touches of body-colour' are often used in descriptions.

As noted, gouache may be bought ready-mixed or it may be prepared by mixing Chinese white with ordinary transparent water-colours during the course of painting. The latter involves little inconvenience and has the advantage that the degree of opacity may be varied. Transparent water-colours may be dry-brushed over gouache to modify underlying hues.

Even the addition of a small quantity of white causes a radical change in the handling qualities and appearance of water-colour. The modified pigment is used in a more or less creamy consistency and applied in short vertical strokes as described in the section on dry-brush. The dilute wash style of typical transparent water-colour is not appropriate, as experiment will show. Coverage is excellent with gouache, enabling large areas of even colour to be built up with few coats. Depending to some extent upon the absorbency of the paper, it is best to avoid thick layers of paint, as these may be disturbed in adding further colours and may also crack or flake.

Any of the supports suitable for water-colour are appropriate for gouache, but less expensive papers and boards may also be used with success. As subjects which suggest the use of gouache are often light-toned, tinted papers are an advantage: the type known as Ingres is ideal.

In appearance a gouache may resemble a like topic treated in acrylics, and the 'feel' in use is not dissimilar in some respects, yet there is one distinctive characteristic in which they differ, which qualifies the use of each. On drying, acrylic colours become water-proof, and virtually limitless coats of differing colours may be added without disturbing the underlayers; but in adding moist pigment to a dried layer, where a blended effect is wanted, the added colour must be brushed out and/or diluted until it merges evenly. This is fairly difficult to do well. In contrast, gouache remains water-soluble when dry, and edges of added colours may be blended softly into their surrounds by using a moist brush-tip to recombine pigment grains.

Gouache is accommodating – mistakes may be painted over, and second thoughts indulged in a way that the discipline imposed by transparent water-colour would not allow. For all that, method is more effective than a random approach; and, as the handling qualities of gouache resemble those of acrylics, the sequence described in detail for acrylics on pp. 134–8 may be helpful.

The poppies (*Papaver* cultivar) illustrated on p. 135 are typical gouache subjects and would make a suitable choice for a first exercise in the medium. For these large light-toned blooms, a tinted (Ingres) paper seemed appropriate: this was heavy enough not to need stretching. Hues were all from the list of transparent water-colours (p. 100) converted to gouache, as each colour mix was prepared, by the addition of Chinese white. Though the other colours were in pans, white was squeezed from a tube each time it was needed, since a white pan would have been constantly sullied.

Drawing was done with a 2B pencil, as the tinted paper required a blacker mark than would have been possible from an HB without damaging pressure. A grade 3 sable brush was used for all but the hairs which were drawn in with a grade 0 sable.

After the pencil drawing was completed, the sequence was as follows:

1 White was used in several layers to build up the petals, with strokes following the venation – that is, radiating from the centre of each bloom. No attempt was made to achieve an overall even tone; rather, the tinted paper underneath was allowed to show through in places to suggest shadow: opposite in effect, but the same in principle, as allowing the white of the support in transparent water-colour to indicate lighter areas.

2 In contrast with the white petals, the unpainted ovaries, capped by stigmatic tissue, then appeared as disconcerting dark holes, so they were put in next using tiny amounts of various greens, blues and yellows mixed with white.

3 Next came the delicate pink of the petal margins. A mixture of alizarin and a touch of vermilion, with lots of white, was blended in by starting each stroke from the petal edge and merging it gently into the underlying coat.

4 Lightly shadowed parts of the petals were then brushed in using the transparent vermilion–ultramarine–yellow shadow mix noted on p. 116; white was not used here as this would have dulled the effect.

5 Having established shadows on the flowers, it was then feasible to show the filaments of the stamens in white against these darker portions. The filaments were then lightly tinted here and there with a brush moistened with dilute transparent green, before being completed by the addition of bright anthers of cadmium yellow brought to opacity by a small amount of white.

6 A first coat of light-toned bright green was then applied to all vegetative parts, using a mixture of sap green, lemon yellow and white. On the leaves this was kept thin enough to allow the pencilled veins to show through.

7 The same mixture was then darkened with more sap green and a little ultramarine for use on the leaves. It was brushed out thinly and blended in with the bright green underlayer on the lighter areas, and allowed to reach full intensity in the darker portions.

8 This colour was adapted for the shaded side of the stems by the introduction of cadmium yellow. A brush-tip just moistened with clean water softened the edge of the shadow.

9 The mixture used in stage 4 was then prepared for deeper shadows throughout. An especially careful touch was needed about the edges of the petals to ensure definition without either halting the shadow build-up too soon or adding rather too much and so giving the almost filmy structures too much weight.

10 The petals were completed by using the faintest tint of dilute transparent cadmium yellow dry-brushed on to suggest a dusting of pollen and reflected colour from the clustered anthers at the centres.

11 On nearing completion, it was clear that the lighter parts of the stems and bud needed heightening: this was done by adding lots of white to a combination of sap green and cadmium yellow.

12 This same mixture was used with yet more white to establish hairs, showing their characteristic downward inclination on all vegetative parts, using a grade 0 sable brush.

13 The final step was the application of the brightest highlights with white modified by a brush-point of ultramarine.

Though topics consisting mainly of light-toned elements may almost demand the use of gouache, it is of course not restricted to this usage. Some artists work almost exclusively in the medium, though perhaps more prefer to switch between the opaque and transparent forms of watercolour according to which best suits the subject in hand.

10 Acrylics

There are several reasons why the botanical artist who works with traditional materials should consider turning to this comparatively recent
medium at least from time to time. These include the manufacturers' claim
that acrylic polymer bound pigments are the 'most permanent medium
for the artist yet created' – an important factor, even though many
water-colours have lasted for hundreds of years without apparent deterioration. For me the great potential of acrylics lies in their flexibility: they
may be diluted with water and used in almost the same way as water-
colours; or, since the colours are waterproof once dry, they may be built
up in transparent layers with as many coats as you wish without fear of the
underlayers breaking up. Pigment may also be applied in a thick impasto:
and glazes and scumbles may then be carried across this surface. Light
colours can be painted over dark with ease, and it is a simple matter to
carry out second thoughts – areas may be painted out and re-established at
will. When used thinly the pigments dry slightly more slowly than
water-colours.

Acrylic colours are ideal for some subjects: plants such as cacti with light
spines against a dark ground, species with lots of white hairs – in fact any
deeply pigmented object bearing light-coloured details. Some of the more
subtle delights of using the medium are not easy to put into words, but
will be discovered if you carry out the exercises described below.

A criticism sometimes used of acrylic colours is that they have a 'plastic'
feel to them. To a degree this is valid where the paints are used in impasto
(though for me this quality is not marked) but not where they are used
thinly as in botanical illustration.

Equipment

ACRYLIC PAINTS Though in one maker's catalogue thirty-eight hues are
offered, I use only twelve colours, including three that haven't been called
on for years. This means that I have been working on and off for a long
period with fewer acrylic pigments than were recommended for the *basic*
water-colour set. I have painted hundreds of plant species using this small
number of hues, without difficulty in mixing required colours other than
the rose-purple mentioned in the last chapter. This is probably because the
ease with which acrylic pigments may be applied in thin successive transparent layers, until the right effect is obtained, allows more or less primary
colours to be used in glazes, each modifying the other so that virtually any
colour may be obtained in this way. With experience, these results can be
planned, as the method allows hints of the underlying colours to show
through in greater or lesser degree, giving a richness to the whole. With
water-colours a more direct approach is preferable to preserve the char-

acteristic freshness of the medium and so hues are mixed from the wider range in an attempt to get them right in one or two moves. Whatever the reason, there is no doubt that fewer colours are needed, and the following basic set is also quite sufficient for all botanical uses: 1 lemon yellow; 2 permanent yellow; 3 cadmium red; 4 crimson; 5 red purple; 6 ultramarine; 7 coeruleum; 8 Hooker's green; 9 white; and a 250 ml tin of white primer.

ADDITIVES It is possible to buy a number of items that may be mixed with acrylic paints for different purposes. There are mediums to give gloss and matt finishes; transparent glazes; water tension breakers; and retarders to slow drying. For most botanical illustration they are not vital. The most useful is the water tension breaker; this may be added when one is working on a poorly absorbent surface and is also helpful in assisting washes to flow on evenly.

VARNISHES If acrylic paintings are to be exposed to the air for lengthy periods in exhibitions etc., they should either be framed behind glass or varnished for protection. When acrylics are used more or less in a water-colour mode, varnish will be inappropriate, and a painting will then be matted and glassed; but where layers of paint have been built up so that the general effect is that of a work in oils, the work is treated accordingly and varnish is then an advantage. Gloss varnish in particular gives an added glow to colours. Protective varnishes for acrylics are removable with white spirit or turpentine.

Though the surface of an acrylic painting framed without glass is tough enough to be cleaned periodically with warm water and a little soap, a protective varnish is strongly advised as cleaning may damage the very thinnest paint layers, especially if a glaze medium has not been used. If a work has been allowed to get dirty, such layers may be obliterated quite unconsciously. For example the artist may in places have quietened a brilliant yellow with a film of transparent grey which could all too easily be removed.

BRUSHES There is little doubt that acrylics shorten brush life. Even when washed out thoroughly they still tend to wear faster than when used for water-colours. For this reason it is sensible to keep separate sets for each medium. A fine quality water-colour brush will last for many years in a near-original state, but the same brush will begin to break down quite quickly if in regular use with acrylics. Unfortunately, cheaper brushes are no solution; the demands of botanical subjects are the same when working in either medium and sable brushes remain without peer for the finest work.

For a selection of brushes, the advice given in chapter 9 applies equally here. An addition worth making for acrylics is a grade 8 flat hog-hair; pigments straight from the tube take a certain amount of manipulation before every particle is dissolved into the diluting water, and this accelerates brush wear; hog-hair is preferable to sable for this operation since it is cheaper and the stiff hairs do a quicker job of mixing. A larger brush, about grade 12, of the same kind, is ideal for use in priming.

SUPPORTS Acrylic paints may be used on almost any surface, excepting a few such as glass where smoothness makes adhesion doubtful. For botanical subjects I prefer a sturdy illustration board instead of paper, though the choice is largely subjective. If the best qualities of acrylics are to be exploited, a heavier ground feels more appropriate. As the medium is so undemanding, you may like to experiment – for example, a hardboard panel lightly sanded and primed gives good results. As noted above, an entirely smooth surface may give problems, but otherwise any rag paper or board, wood, hardboard, canvas or other fabric may be found suitable if it possesses a slight tooth or grain. As with water-colour, light-weight papers should be stretched to avoid cockling.

PALETTES Disposable palettes of white tear-off sheets are available, but I favour a white china plate – its shape permits wetter mixes to be made in the recessed base portion, which can afterwards be wiped clean with a paper towel; the rim is ideal for arranging dabs of colour straight from the tubes and for mixing small amounts of dryish pigment. Its white colour allows other hues to be seen without distortion, and it is easily cleaned after use – dried paint peels away freely under hot water.

Once acrylics dry they become waterproof, and when mixed colours are needed for a lengthy task this can be a nuisance. Where for instance a number of leaves are to receive the same undercolour, if the pigment is mixed on the flat surface of the plate it will dry before the coat is completed: at least the edges will almost certainly congeal to be picked up by the brush and deposited on the painting as fragments. There are two solutions: a commercial retarder will slow drying significantly but is tricky to use because if a mistake is made in the amount added – 6 drops to 2.5 cm (1 in.) of pigment is the rule – the reverse effect occurs and drying is hastened. When only 5 mm ($\frac{3}{16}$ in.) of paint is required, it is easy to squeeze out too many drops of retardant. The more acceptable solution is to slow the rate of evaporation by mixing larger amounts of paint into high-sided narrow-mouthed containers; an ideal size is about 6 cm ($2\frac{1}{2}$ in.) in diameter and 3.5 cm ($1\frac{1}{2}$ in.) high. This reduces the area of surface exposed to moving air, and even a shallow layer of pigment at the bottom will last in usable condition for hours rather than the minutes that would have been available otherwise. The life of the mix may be further extended if the jar is covered.

WATER-JAR The same criteria apply as for water-colour.

LIGHT-WEIGHT DRAWING-BOARD This will be needed for the purpose described in the previous chapter, unless stiff heavy-weight supports are used.

MISCELLANEOUS In the main the same items needed for water-colours are also useful here; in addition, if you prefer primed surfaces, a few hard pencils, 3H to 6H, should be included: priming paint creates an abrasive ground which takes the sharp point from softer pencils too quickly – in making outlines a 3H or even harder pencil will behave much as an HB does on a more yielding surface.

Techniques

If you intend to use acrylics more or less as water-colours, you will find that most of the techniques described in chapter 9 may be applied: though as acrylics dry waterproof, the methods for lifting off paint to remove errors and to put in venation or highlights cannot be used.

To get the best from acrylics, you should not use them as substitutes for water-colours, or for oils for that matter. The medium should be enjoyed for its own strengths, explored below. Acrylics may also be used in an impasto with or without the aid of a palette knife, but this technique is generally outside the requirements of botanical topics and is mentioned only in passing as a possible option for special purposes.

PRIMING This is a good point at which to test the difference between working on a primed surface and an unprimed one. Much depends upon the type of support used and personal preference. The colour trial exercise described below may be carried out on both primed and unprimed board so that your own assessment may be made. Once the priming is completed, it takes little time to repeat the exercise on an unprimed surface while waiting for coats to dry. Thick card or illustration board is suitable as this will provide a hard-wearing record.

The object of priming is to create a sealed surface which will bond with colours while not allowing them to be taken into the underlying support. Colours applied thinly on a primed material will dry with a faint semi-gloss, whereas the same mixture used on an unprimed surface may sink in to dry with a matt finish. The difference in effect is slight, and depends a good deal upon variables, but some highly absorbent supports are often clearly improved by priming, as are some hard non-absorbent grounds upon which a first coat of colour may be slow to establish. Though priming before a painting is started may seem tedious, it is quickly done.

White priming paint should be applied with the grade 12 hog-hair brush. Dilute the pigment with water to a thin creamy consistency, thin enough to dry without leaving brush marks yet thick enough not to run too freely down the tilted board; a slope of about 30° is again convenient. Even though acrylics are best used in a slightly less dilute form than water-colour, a slanted surface allows the pigment to move down the sheet which helps in achieving an even coat. Do not go back over any area which is semi-dry as the surface will then be marked with brush strokes – this is a general rule when using acrylics. To avoid moving into partly dry paint when priming a large area, sections should be primed in turn as shown in fig. 81. By the time the moist lower working edge of each section is carried down to the bottom of the sheet, the top edge adjoining the next section should be touch dry. Two or three thin coats usually give a better finish than one thick one. Though no difficulty will be found in seeing the progress of the first layer of white paint against the white ground, due to differences in whiteness and texture, it is sometimes not easy to see where sections of subsequent coats begin and end. This is overcome by putting a pencil mark on the furthest margin of each section. After the first coat, which is absorbed and dried quickly, subsequent layers may remain moist rather longer.

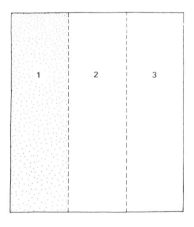

81 Priming in sections (left-handed persons should reverse the sequence)

Enough layers of primer must be used to ensure that there are no missed portions however small, otherwise a blotchy effect will result when paint inside such 'windows' is absorbed more readily and these spots will stand out as being slightly darker than their surrounds. Too many coats of primer create another problem: though the primer film should be smooth and unmarked by brush-strokes, if the layers are too thick they may completely fill the minute depressions that form the tooth or grain of the support. This will create a slick surface on which diluted colours may be dislodged by brush pressure when further coats are added. You will generally be conscious of the possibility of super-smoothness creeping in and stop priming well short of this point, but sometimes paint will 'take' better on some parts than on others, and tooth may disappear from these areas well in advance of the rest. The remedy is to use yet more primer on the offending places, using less dilution so that the stiffer pigment can be 'teased' and worked with the brush to a finely textured finish.

COLOUR RECORD A sensible first step is to provide a permanent record of the appearance of each colour, much as was done with water-colour. Again, a number of panels should be drawn up so that each colour may be represented, plus a few extra to allow for later purchases. However, for acrylics, as white is added on occasion as a means of lightening a colour (rather than to change the mode of use, as in transmuting water-colour to gouache), enough panels should be drawn so that the effect of adding white may be demonstrated on the same sheet as the pure colours.

Hues may be put down in the same order as in the list on p. 128 to give a convenient progression from yellows through reds and blues etc.

When the priming has been completed and the required numbers of panels have been drawn for the first exercise on both the primed and the unprimed boards, painting can begin. As panels will remain moist for some minutes, enough of each colour should be mixed to allow four or five rectangles to be painted at a time. When the last in the sequence receives its first layer, the initial one will be dry and waiting for a second coat. Allow half or so of each area to remain with one or at most two coats while the rest is built up until the hue reaches maximum intensity; you will then have a record of the appearance of each colour in two strengths.

Colours should be fairly well diluted though not quite to the same extent as a water-colour wash. A very slight creaminess should remain. Add the paint with a grade 3 brush using short vertical strokes from top to bottom of each panel, working from side to side. The first coat usually dries with an even finish, but if there happen to be a few small blemishes these will be obscured as additional layers are put down, until each colour at full intensity is represented by an area without flaw.

PASTEL SHADES The next step is to see how colours behave when white is added to lighten them. As in gouache, the pigments become opaque and fewer coats are needed to reach maximum strength. These pastel shades are invaluable in creating *large* even areas of colours at a lessened density. Though lighter versions of colours are achieved, they lose something of their brilliance – and for small areas the direct route of watered down colour is perhaps the best as the quality of the hue is unimpaired. However, when the colour to be matched is itself a pastel shade the addition of white is the most appropriate approach.

As noted above, *large* areas of colours used at less than full intensity are best achieved by the use of pigment admixed with white. But it is difficult to control a big area of diluted colour in acrylics because edges dry in hard lines that are impossible to take out (though see also p. 137). A water-colour wash technique is also unsatisfactory since acrylics used in this way generally do not dry completely evenly, particularly on primed board. Yet in spite of these reservations, problems are not often encountered – the working area for a botanical subject is usually small enough to be tackled directly without a white admixture.

There are several points to make about pastel shades. Where the admixture of white has caused loss of brilliance, it is often possible partly to recover this by adding a thin overlayer of pure colour. Provided small sections are handled at a time this may be very successful. Another feature is that though acrylic colours in general tend to dry marginally darker (in contrast to water-colour) than they are when wet, this is more marked when white is a component. When, for example, a leaf painted in a pastel green is darkened by adding a slightly deeper hue still containing white, it is difficult to assess the amount of pigment needed to reach the correct tone for the new mix: you will find the darker colour hard to apply so that the edges brush out to make a smooth transition into the paler area, because when wet the edges will appear to dissolve into the surround, only to be glaringly visible as they dry. The solution, when working with colours containing a significant proportion of white, is to work from *dark* to *light*, rather than from mid-tones to dark and then back to light as detailed below.

COLOUR MIXING As mentioned in the water-colour chapter, if *pure* primary colours were available to the artist, very few pigments would be required; but as this is not the case, it is as well to be familiar with likely results from elementary mixes, especially the sequence moving from red, yellow and blue (primaries), to orange, purple and green (secondaries). The secondaries are obtained by equal mixtures of the pairs: yellow + red, red + blue, blue + yellow, respectively. Lemon yellow is close to being a primary colour, but the available blues and reds lie on either side of the primaries cyan and magenta – and it is worth exploring all the following combinations to obtain a record of the various results.

1 Lemon yellow + cadmium red, cadmium red + coeruleum, coeruleum + lemon yellow.

2 Lemon yellow + crimson, crimson + ultramarine, ultramarine + lemon yellow.

3 Lemon yellow + crimson, crimson + coeruleum, coeruleum + lemon yellow.

The last example contains some duplications, but the combinations are best carried through in sequence (fig. 82) in order to see the complete

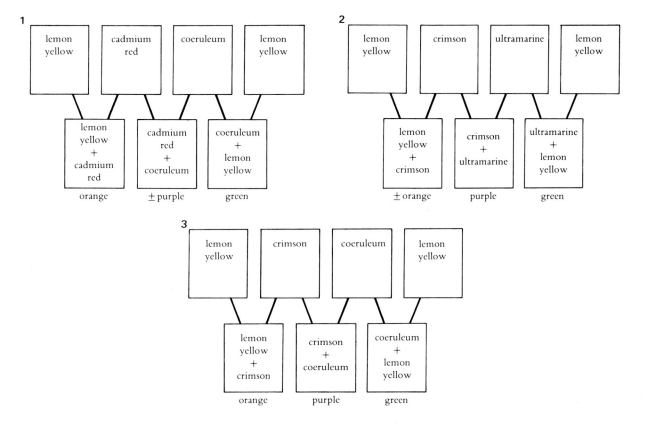

movement from near-primary colours to secondary colours in each instance.

82 Colour mixtures

Note the differences in character of the secondary colours, depending upon the reds, blues and yellows chosen. In the first set the orange and green are clear and fresh; but the purple is quite close to brown, because the red and the blue in this instance both have a slightly yellow bias which contaminates what otherwise could have been a pure purple. Similarly, in the second example the orange is unsatisfactory due to the hint of blue in crimson, and the green is dulled because ultramarine contains red. The purple here is rather better than the first example yet still far from the clear colour often required. In the final set the orange and the green have been repeated from the other combinations, the purple is new, and this also has been spoiled, this time through the presence of yellow in coeruleum.

The process can be carried further by mixing combinations of secondary colours, and of secondaries and primaries. Unexpected colours may be produced until the habit of analysis is acquired. For instance, when you recognize that the failure to produce a good purple from the equal mixture of cadmium red and coeruleum is due to the presence of yellow in these colours, and that this contaminant in fact creates a colour close to a chocolate brown, you will see that the familiar 'red and green make brown' may also be expressed as 'red, blue and yellow make brown provided that the correct quantities of each are used'. And, of course, since the amounts required in all colour mixes depend upon the characteristics of the reds, blues and yellows concerned, it is helpful to think of each of these in terms of their relationship to pure primaries.

Though you will discover many useful colours through the above experiments, they will not include a purple of sufficient purity to be used either on its own or in combinations to paint flowers in the red-purple range. Red-purple is a colour that has to be purchased. My own is satisfactory when used on its own though it tends to become leaden when mixed with other hues, and it is also too opaque: these qualities can be to some degree neutralized by using it as a base colour which may be modified by transparent glazes of other hues – a solution similar to that described for water-colour (p. 119) in obtaining a purplish-blue.

As with water-colour, an excellent black may be achieved by the combination of red and blue with a touch of yellow, and variations of this mixture in dilute form provide basic shadow colours. A preferred recipe for shadow colours is roughly equal parts of cadmium red and ultramarine, though the red may be replaced by crimson where a slightly less grey quality is needed.

To assess the effect obtained by using each colour in turn as an underlayer and as a modifying glaze, try the same exercise in acrylics as was described for water-colours (fig. 80). The aim is to show each colour as it appears underneath and on top of each of the other colours.

The exercises so far, though fairly time-consuming, will provide a useful permanent record; but there will doubtless be some readers who will be content simply to read about trying out their colours without going so far as to carry out the work. Yet the novice in this medium might use even more time getting to know how the paints behave by doodling in an unstructured way than by carrying out the suggested first steps.

PAINTING METHOD Whether or not these trials have been completed, I would urge you to follow the next procedure – the principle of working from light to mid-tone to dark, then from dark to light – as it forms the core of much botanical work in this medium.

The portion of the leaf on p. 136 is a convenient topic to use in acquiring foundation techniques. In this instance it may be better to copy the illustration than to look for a leaf showing all the characteristics included. The steps given below, though also applicable to a host of non-botanical subjects, are ones which I adopt almost invariably in working on plants. From the point when the drawing is completed (in HB pencil on unprimed and 4-6H on primed board) the sequence is as follows:

1 Lightest tones. Assess the lightest *local* colour present: that is, the actual colour of the plant, or portion of the plant, that is lightest in tone, ignoring transitory effects of the light which may produce highlights or bright areas. Frequently the lightest-toned colour will be found on stems, petioles, veins etc. Where this colour covers a significant area, difficult to define here but usually obvious in practice, it is generally sensible to paint it first, using well diluted pigment. Such portions can be put in later, but leaving them white and hence over-bright until the final stages often creates a slight problem in maintaining a correct tonal balance. In the illustration

OPPOSITE
Gouache: poppies, *Papaver* cultivar

Keith West

the veins were the lightest local colour and were established first with a grade 3 sable (used throughout) in a thin mixture of greenish-yellow.

2 Middle tones. The basic overall colour underlying both shadows and highlights may be thought of as a 'middle tone'. (As used here the term does not describe a tone mid-way between black and white as shown in the scale on fig. 13 – though it may coincidentally be so – but refers to the middle tone of a particular subject. In this context a light-coloured leaf will have a middle tone above the mid-point on the absolute scale, and a dark-coloured leaf will have a middle tone below the mid-point. The ambiguity exists only in writing – the concept presents no problems in the actual work sequence. You may prefer the term 'ground-colour', or perhaps 'underlying colour', yet these also are faintly ambiguous.) The green used as the middle tone in the illustration, a mixture of Hooker's green and a little permanent yellow, was brushed thinly over the whole illustration except the veins. The areas between the veins and the bounds of the illustration formed convenient sections to work in, removing any concern about the moist leading edge of the pigment drying. Almost always an element of planning in this respect is sensible, to avoid having to hide lines of dried pigment. If this seems likely the edge in question should be brushed out so that it fades into the white support surface. A thin paint layer can be blended in later to leave little or no blemish.

More often than not leaves etc. present faintly mottled colours, but if the subject demands a perfectly even middle-tone, a cautious approach using several thin coats is recommended.

3 Darker tones. The middle tone dried almost immediately with such a thin paint film, and the same mix was then used to darken the areas running in to shadow. This procedure is tricky and often calls for the use of a finger-tip as well as the brush. Strokes were applied leading away from the light – from right to left in the illustration. A right-hander might find it easier to turn the board around and reverse the movements. The aim was to start the darkening process from the points on the leaf which appeared gradually to deepen in tone as the surface curved out of the light, and to make the transition so smooth that the beginning of the change was imperceptible. The action of stroking the brush away from the light carries pigment in the same direction, and this helps to blend in the leading edge. Often this is not enough and the merging of the layers has to be assisted by mopping up excess around the point at which each blending stroke begins. This must be done with speed before the pigment begins to settle in, and the only practicable tool that I have found to do the job is the tip of a free finger on the same hand that holds the brush. Three or four blending strokes with the brush are made, moving down the sheet, the finger-tip is then used to dab away a minute amount of moist paint, and because the area is still damp, pigment from the wetter parts of the strokes will ease back partially into the blotted bits to aid in blending. The dabbing action has to be fast to allow the paint to be brushed to its destination before drying: in this case to a vein or the boundary of the leaf. Drying pigment should not be allowed to build up on the finger or crumbs of paint will eventually break away and transfer to the work.

OPPOSITE ABOVE
An example of work in acrylics: dandelion, *Taraxacum officinale*

BELOW
Leaf section (magnified) demonstrating acrylic technique

Each section was completed in this way, moving down the sheet three or four strokes at a time. One darkening coat is seldom enough, and for this illustration three were used, each beginning a fraction further away from the light. Finally, for the deepest shadow, the green hue reached its maximum intensity – additional layers would then have altered only the thickness of the film without other visible effect.

4 Shadows. With the broad areas of light and shade defined, the study still looked rather dull. It is at this stage that the fun really begins. The next move was to deepen the shadows yet further by adding to the dark areas a shadow mixture of more or less equal parts of cadmium red and ultramarine well diluted. This was brushed on thinly as described for step 3. Though small imperfections in blending were lost in the surrounding deep tone, the use of a finger-tip was still needed here and there. As noted for water-colour, except on very pale surfaces and in the darkest areas, shadow colour should not be evident. In the leaf portion illustrated the deep shadows are not seen as a distinct colour, just a hint of purple in the green, yet their presence makes a major difference in bringing the leaf surface to life.

5 Modifiers. The next phase is the introduction of colours to modify underlayers that have not worked quite as planned, or simply to suggest overlying hues – as in the present exercise where parts are suffused with a hint of warmth. A watered-down cadmium red was used which gave an effect of chestnut brown owing to the green under-colour showing through.

The veins then received another coat; this contained white to render the greenish-yellow more opaque, with the intention of breaking and blurring the hard green edges. The paint was mixed to a fairly thick consistency and put on in tiny dabs which were worked with the brush-point until the required effect was gained. The veins then appeared too chalky because of the added white and so were modified by the thinnest glaze of dilute permanent yellow followed by a little shadow colour. The cadmium red mix was used towards the base of the midrib to give a further lively touch. This time the red acquired an orange tinge through the presence of yellow in the midvein. Note that the cadmium red yielded two colour effects: chestnut over green, and orange over yellow.

6 Highlights. The final step was to define the highlights by blending in a mix of white with a hint of coeruleum. They were slowly brought to full intensity by putting on the pigment in layers using a lightly loaded brush. This was first tested on the protective sheet until each stroke left only a ghost-faint mark. For the brightest part of each highlight extra white was added.

As this sequence is basic to the practice of botanical illustration in acrylics, it will be found helpful for virtually all plant subjects. When you have mastered the above technique you will be equipped for a full-scale topic such as that shown on p. 136.

The subject chosen for this illustration is the widely available dandelion, *Taraxacum officinale*. After the quite complex drawing had been completed, the painting progressed as follows – the sequence being in accord with that described for the last exercise. A grade 3 brush was used throughout, except where a finer tip was needed for minute detail.

1 A pale green mix of dilute ultramarine and permanent yellow established the leaf midribs and the stems of the flowering/fruiting heads.

2 Bright translucent leaf areas were then suggested, using a light-toned lime-green mixed from Hooker's green and permanent yellow.

3 A middle-tone (see p. 137) green mixed from Hooker's green, permanent yellow, ultramarine, and cadmium red formed the basic coat for the leaves. This was blended in to skirt the edges of the translucent portions.

4 Second and third coats of the same mix were applied to darken parts of the leaves to show modelling.

5 Green sections of the flower, the fruiting head and the bud towards the plant base, were put in, modifying the mixture of step 3 with touches of various other colours as required.

6 A satisfactory brown for the clustered fruits of the dandelion 'clock' was also obtained from the step 3 mix by adding crimson and a hint of ultramarine.

7 The feathery *pappus* of the 'clock' had been indicated earlier in very faint pencil in the under-drawing. This was lightly reinforced in paint, using a much diluted shadow mixture of cadmium red and ultramarine modified by permanent yellow – avoiding the already painted fruits and reflexed bracts. Where the pappus passed over these portions it was defined by a network of fine white lines applied with a grade 0 brush.

8 The same shadow mixture was also used on darker portions of the flower head; it was then painted over with a transparent mixture of permanent yellow and lemon yellow, using several coats to build up intensity in parts. To gain the richer hue of the capitulum centre, a minute amount of cadmium red was added to the yellows.

9 Dilute crimson was used for the tips of the *phyllaries*, the lower midribs of the leaves and the peduncles.

10 Shadowed portions throughout were put in with the mix of step 7, with a succession of several layers to approach black in the darkest places.

11 Highlights of white qualified by coeruleum blue (applied as described in the last exercise) added the final lively touches throughout.

11 Photography

As I stressed in chapter 2, I am concerned here with photography as an aid to botanical illustration – as a means of recording information about a subject when, for a variety of reasons, it may not be easily obtainable from live material. Any advice given is therefore relevant only to this aspect of taking photographs and is not intended as a guide to plant photography for its own sake.

Choice of camera brand and general instruction in camera use are beyond the range of this book, but most libraries will have lots of books covering these topics. The best kind of camera for botanical work is a single lens reflex (SLR) with either a macro-lens or a set of close-up lenses. A camera of this type is expensive, and so is a macro-lens. Close-up lenses are relatively cheap and will do a perfectly adequate job, though it is annoying to have continually to put them on and take them off when working on a number of species at a time.

A primary consideration is whether to use colour prints or colour transparencies. Transparencies record colour much more accurately but are too small to work from. This can be overcome with a device consisting of a miniature screen, housed in a cabinet, on to which a slide is back-projected so that you can sit close to it and work directly from the enlarged image. Though convenient, this aid is expensive for limited or infrequent use. My own choice is to use colour prints: they can be handled quite roughly, stored easily, and if sensible field practice has been followed (see below) measurements may be taken off and converted as required. They do, however, deteriorate over the years.

A high-speed film is helpful. Though the larger grain size can minutely affect detail, this is not discernible unless exposures have been made in poor light. ASA/ISO 400 colour print film is sold from most outlets and this allows photography in conditions from brilliant sunlight to deep shade. This flexibility may well be needed in the kinds of circumstances that make photography necessary: in mountains, for example, changes in light during the course of a day may be extreme. Another virtue of fast film is that it will permit photography in the windiest conditions – with an exposure of 1/500 sec. and above, even the most wildly whipping plant will be frozen crisply – if you can keep it in focus. A partner can help to some extent in providing shelter, though if much work is to be done in strong winds, the construction of a screen may be called for. I have not found a tripod essential in photographing plants. The purpose of a tripod is to avoid blurring due to camera-shake – and this problem is largely overcome by using high-speed film. There are occasions when a high f-stop is needed to gain maximum depth of field, and this, depending on lighting, may entail a fairly long exposure – but if one can move into a position in which the camera is firmly braced without the kind of tension that leads to quivering, then excellent results may still be obtained even with exposures of up to 1/8 sec. However, exposures of longer than 1/60 sec. are risky, and if a tripod is available it should certainly then be used. Many SLR cameras have a self-timer, which is worthwhile when exposures of 1/60 sec. or longer are involved as it removes the danger of jarring the camera when pressing the shutter-release button. A flash attachment solves the problem of poor lighting but usually this is not vital.

Many plant photographers find a tripod indispensable because they view flowers more often than not from above. But the botanical artist's camera work is usually done from a position where each section of the plant in question is viewed at eye-level. Unless one is working on taller species, a great deal of time is spent lying down. In this position the body can act as a tripod. The camera, pressed gently against the face, forms the apex of a triangle described by the fore-arms and the distance between the elbows as they rest on the ground; the upper arms and shoulders also give firm support. The height of the camera above the ground may be adjusted by moving the elbows further apart or closer together.

Each exposure should be recorded in a notebook with all relevant details. These will include the species name, the part of the plant photographed – whole habit, upper, mid, lower, inflorescence, detail of flower, detail of calyx, detail of leaf from mid-stem, and so forth. Rapid sketches may be needed here and there to help with details that experience teaches will be obscured on the print – for example, light-coloured stamens and/or stigmas. As colour prints invariably drift towards the blue or the red ends of the spectrum, notes should be taken about critical hues. Probably the most accurate method is to quote from the 800 colour variants shown in the excellent Royal Horticultural Society colour chart; though recording may also be conveniently done by using colour-pencils; or by noting the actual pigment names in the medium to be used for the finished illustration. If film can be processed and printed quickly, it is worthwhile to compare the print with the living plant; colour notes may then be added lightly to the back of the print to indicate the amount of drift that has occurred. In any case, two visits to a locality are often needed, as there will always be one or two exposures that would be better repeated. This problem might be overcome by using one of the newer polaroid-type cameras, but detailed colour notes will be essential.

The light of early morning and evening has a reddish cast which is recorded by sensitive film; yet there are situations where one is obliged to work at these times – prairies and coasts, for instance, may breed vicious winds around mid-day that make photographing flowers, especially those on slender springy stems, all but impossible. On these occasions extra care should be taken to make accurate colour notes.

Plant photographs are best taken when the sun is partly screened by a thinnish layer of cloud – not too thick otherwise shady spots, forest interiors and the like, will become too dark, but just enough to blur hard-edged shadows.

Sometimes there is little choice, and one should be aware of the likely effects of working in direct sunlight. Deep shadows contrast over-strongly with the lighted surrounds, so that if exposure is correct for the lighter portions, the shadows will appear on the print as indecipherable black areas. And, if the shadowed parts are correctly exposed, sun-splashed pieces will be burnt into white splodges. Averaged exposures may be more or less satisfactory; but exposures ranging over several f-stops provide a better hope of success. In bright sunlight even slightly glossy leaves will lose local colour and become pale blue in reflecting the sky, and colours on the whole may seem slightly washed out. A polarizing filter should cut reflected light to an acceptable level.

There are other ways of negating the worst effects of direct sun. A companion can stand so as to throw a shadow over the subject provided that the plant is small enough, but make sure that no splash of sunshine remains visible through the viewfinder, as this could distort the exposure somewhat, or at least ruin what otherwise could have been a pleasing print. A colourless translucent plastic sheet may also be useful on occasion to diffuse the sun's rays; and where shadows are too contrasty, a fill-in light may be introduced by placing a white piece of cardboard on the shadowy side of the subject to serve as a reflector.

A recurrent problem when photographing flowers in close-up is that of capturing the details of white or light-coloured blooms backed by dark foliage; this is related to the difficulty mentioned above of adequately treating subjects involving high contrast through the juxtaposition of sunlight and shadow. The solution is much the same: to make exposures over several f-stops. To ensure that all-important floral details are rendered clearly it is as well to include one or two frames that are distinctly underexposed. This is best done by turning the f-stop ring to a higher number than that indicated by the exposure meter, so reducing the aperture and hence light entry (another way is to increase shutter-speed, but that is slightly more fiddly). The prints will probably show flowers somewhat greyed and surrounded by amorphous gloom, but features such as stamens, stigmas etc. should be well-defined; faint colouring often seen in petal-tips, ovaries and so on (which might vanish with a 'normal' exposure) may then be decipherable if one mentally strips off the shadowy overlying grey, and even such minutiae as petal venation may be captured. The reduced aperture also increases depth of field.

Each exposure should be recorded as it is made; it is almost impossible to remember details later. It is invaluable to have a partner to carry out this work – notes are inclined to be much more complete if they may be dictated while each operation is carried through.

Measurements must be taken for each plant even though voucher specimens are also collected where possible: distortion in dried specimens sometimes makes accurate measurement and the identification of a particular organ photographed next to impossible. Every exposure entered in the notebook should be accompanied by at least one measurement. In each case dimensions taken can be correlated with those present in the photograph – and this gives a key to all dimensions in each print. For example, a flower detail photographed in close-up measures 4.45 cm across on the living plant; the same feature on the print might be perhaps 6.6 cm. By calculation it will be found that any dimension on the print will be restored to its measure in life (in perspective) when multiplied by a factor of 0.67: that is, if 6.6 cm on the photo equals 4.45 cm on the subject, $1 = 4.45/6.6 = 0.67$. (The same principle can, of course, be applied to measurements in inches.) The use of the memory function of a pocket calculator for repeated multiplication by the same factor is recommended. It is preferable to take too many measurements rather than too few, as sometimes dimensions that otherwise appear almost superfluous may be used to check others where an error is suspected.

A convenient instrument for taking measurements is a metal spring-loaded pocket tape marked to millimetres or tenths of an inch.

As noted on p. 30, voucher specimens should always be taken when work is being done for a scientific purpose. Such specimens become doubly helpful when it is necessary to use photographs in making an illustration.

It is wise to protect the camera when working in harsh conditions. An ultra-violet filter kept permanently in place means that scratches and other damage will be sustained by the inexpensive filter rather than the expensive lens. It is good practice in rough country to keep the camera in a small pack on the back to minimize the chances of having it swing against rocks, trees etc., and also to keep it from the heat of the sun's rays which may be damaging in warmer climates.

Photographs in the studio are poor substitutes for living plants; yet good quality prints, backed up by notes, sketches and voucher specimens, may be sufficient for many purposes, as an aid towards illustration, especially when informed by experience and botanical knowledge.

In emphasizing that photographs at best can never be as valuable as live models I do not intend to devalue botanical photography as a mode of illustration in itself; as discussed in the Introduction, there is a place for the botanical artist and for the photographer. It is simply that the artist obliged to rely upon photographs is, even though aided by supplementary material, still largely limited to the information gathered through the lens – which is inevitably of a lower order than that to be taken from living tissue.

12 Preparing for the printer

If your work is to be reproduced, a knowledge of printing processes will be helpful and may be acquired from references such as Steinberg's *Five Hundred Years of Printing*, or the entry under 'Printing' in more recent editions of *The New Encyclopaedia Britannica*.

When illustrations are to appear in a particular journal, note the standard of reproduction shown in previous issues. It is senseless to use the finest detail when the printer is capable only of reproducing the coarsest of lines. Don't modify quality but do use an appropriate medium and technique.

You will be briefed as to whether to work in black and white or colour. Few scientific journals will print in colour unless colour is vital to the author's thesis, and even then this may depend on current economic conditions. Colour is still common in plant books of wide appeal such as those for the amateur botanist and the gardener, and fine prints of plant paintings remain popular.

REDUCTION AND ALIGNMENT Some illustrations will be in demand again and again, and recurrent use may pose difficulties of size and reduction. Diagrammatic rough sketches done at poster scale to illustrate a lecture have later appeared in a journal much reduced but still legible, then further reduced and quite illegible in a bulletin. As far as you can, try to retain control over the degree of reduction that your work receives. This is most important with line-drawings in ink destined for letterpress reproduction. Usually one-third reduction is suitable for drawings with fine lines; one-half reduction may be extreme. Photolithography can handle reductions greater than fifty per cent but the effects are difficult to visualize.

The printer will find it helpful if you put small 'L' shaped register marks in the corners of each plate – these will assist in placing the illustration in an upright position on the page. Dimensions between the marks should bear a relationship to the image area of the printed page. For example if the image area (that is, the area of the page actually covered by print) is 15×11 cm ($6 \times 4\frac{1}{3}$ in.) and your drawing has been done with a one-third reduction in mind for a full-page, then the dimensions between the marks should measure 22.5×16.5 cm ($9 \times 6\frac{1}{2}$ in.). The required printed size of the horizontal dimension may also be written lightly in pencil just below the lower pair of register marks; the printer will not usually need any other instructions on the plate, and the pencil marks are easily removed when the illustrations are returned. The above procedure should be discussed with the editor or printer as there may be 'house-rules' to observe.

A few plant illustrations look almost equally well placed upright, lying down, or even upside-down, and it is wise to indicate 'top' or 'bottom' in pencil on any work that may be misinterpreted.

LETTERING AND SCALE   The printer may be asked to add lettering of an appropriate style to a plate; though more often instant transfer is put on by the artist. Lettering should be chosen with the amount of reduction in mind – in general, after printing, it should not appear larger than the type used for the text.

The manner of indicating the scale of an illustration will often leave room for choice. Sometimes a plate will require several different scales: the main portion, a plant habit perhaps, will be drawn at life-size or similar; dissections and like details may be magnified; hair-types etc. may be shown much enlarged – up to ×100 or so. There are two main methods of recording magnification. A series of plates of a single scale placed together in the text may be covered by a single note ('all figures ×2' – or whatever) at a point prior to their insertion, or the scale may be included in the individual captions. Alternatively, scales may appear on the plate itself alongside the subject or grouped in some way.

Magnification signs are open to error. When included in a note in the text, it is not unknown for that note to be omitted. Nor is it unknown for the dimensions of the publication, and so that of the plates, to be changed after preparation of the illustrations and the text: so where accuracy is most critical, it is lost. A neat single-line bar scale expressed in centimetres, millimetres or microns, is the best answer. If several such scales are to appear on one plate it may be convenient to group them in a corner as shown in fig. 65; the degree of magnification then remains on the illustration and will be valid no matter how much the size of the setting is changed.

Scales are often too heavy and obtrusive – they should not be allowed to dominate, though at the same time they should be easy to locate and to read.

PRESENTATION   It is sound to present your creations as having some value. If work is grubby and without a protective cover when it is handed to the purchaser, author, editor or printer, it will be treated with the same lack of respect. Plates sent away in a manila folder bearing the request 'Please do not mark originals' are generally returned in good order. Sets of drawings, if small, should be placed in one container cut to size; if, say, full-page then it is best to give each plate its own folder and to provide a container for the set. For mailing, use *rigid* corrugated cardboard sheets to protect both front and back, cut so that the grooves of each sheet run in opposite directions to give extra stiffness and strength. Make sure that the name of the project – book, monograph, paper etc. – is marked lightly in pencil on the back of each illustration and more prominently on the container, which should also carry a return address.

It may be a considerable time after your illustrations have been sent away that they eventually appear in print: usually several months; occasionally longer. Other than for the smallest contributions you should receive a copy or copies. For some works it is sensible for the artist to collaborate with the printer – and then the opportunity may be available to obtain 'pulls'. Such examples of published illustrations should be saved to use in building a portfolio of impressive plant portraits.

Glossary of botanical terms used in the text

Some terms have several meanings: only those applicable to the particular usages in the text are included here.

Abscission The dropping away of plant parts, leaves etc.

Achene A simple dry one-seeded indehiscent fruit (fig. 32*h*). See also *Capsule, Follicle, Nut.*

Actinomorphic Used of a radially symmetrical or regular flower having more than one plane of symmetry (fig. 36 *d, e, f, h*).

Alternate Leaves, buds etc. placed singly along an axis or stem without being opposite or whorled.

Angiosperms Plant group in which seeds are borne within a matured ovary (fruit). See also *Gymnosperms.*

Androecium The male elements collectively, the stamens (fig. 35). See also *Gynoecium.*

Anther The pollen-bearing part of the stamen (fig. 35).

Areole A small pit or raised area, often carrying a tuft of hairs, glochids or spines.

Armature Collectively, barbs, hooks, prickles and spines on a plant.

Axil The upper angle between a branch(let), leaf or leafstalk (petiole), flower-stalk (peduncle or pedicel), and the stem from which it grows.

Axis The main or central line of development of any plant or organ; the main stem.

Basidiocarp A type of fungal 'fruiting' body such as the mushroom (fig. 15*a*).

Basifixed Attached by the base, as anthers may be joined to filaments (fig. 44*a*). See also *Dorsifixed.*

Berry Fleshy fruit which includes one or more carpels and seeds, but no true stone – grapes, tomatoes etc. (fig. 32*b*). See also *Drupe, Pome.*

Bract A modified, usually reduced leaf-like structure on an inflorescence.

Bud An embryonic shoot.

Bulb An underground storage organ comprised of fleshy scale leaves on a short axis (fig. 29*a*). See also *Corm.*

Bullate Blistered or puckered.

Bundle scar Mark on leaf scar left by vascular bundles at the time of leaf abscission (Fig. 26). See also *Leaf scar, Vascular.*

Calyx Sepals collectively. The outside floral whorl (fig. 42*a*).

Capitulum A close inflorescence of aggregated and usually sessile flowers in a compact head, as in a daisy (fig. 37).

Capsule A dehiscent dry fruit developed from two or more carpels (fig. 32*c, d*). See also *Achene, Follicle, Nut.*

Carpel An organ in angiosperms that encloses one or more ovules; a member of the gynoecium (fig. 35).

Carpellate Possessing or composed of carpels.

Column Structure found in orchids formed through union of stamens, styles and stigmas (fig. 43).

Compound leaf A leaf of two or more leaflets (fig. 16*d*).

Corm An erect bulb-like part of the stem as seen in *Crocus* and *Gladiolus*. See also *Bulb.*

Corolla Petals collectively.

Cotyledon Seed leaf. See also *Monocotyledon, Dicotyledon.*

Dehiscence The process of opening in an anther or fruit; hence *dehiscent* and *indehiscent* (not opening).

Dentate With sharp spreading coarse teeth, perpendicular to the margin.

Dicotyledon One of the two classes of angiosperms. Plants in this group have embryos with two cotyledons. See also *Cotyledon, Monocotyledon.*

Digitate Handlike, compound with elements originating from one point.

Disc florets The tubular actinomorphic flowers composing the central portions of flower heads of most Asteraceae (aster family or Compositae, composites) (fig. 37). See also *Ray florets.*

Dioecious Having staminate (male) and pistillate (female) flowers borne separately on different individual plants. See also *Monoecious.*

Dorsifixed Attached by the back, as anthers may be joined to filament (fig. 44*b*). See also *Basifixed.*

Drupe Fleshy fruit, with one seed enclosed by a hard covering; stone fruit (fig. 32*g*). See also *Berry, Pome.*

Entire With a continuous margin lacking teeth or indentations (fig. 19*a*).

Epigynous With sepals, petals and stamens apparently growing from the top of the ovary. See also *Hypogynous, Perigynous.*

Falls Outer whorl of perianth parts in an *Iris* flower (fig. 40).

Family The taxonomic group between order and genus.

Filament The stalk of a stamen (fig. 35).

Floral tube A cup or tube formed by the fusion of the basal parts of sepals, petals and stamens.

Floret Individual flower, especially of composites and grasses (fig. 37).

Follicle A dry, dehiscent fruit opening along one side, derived from a single carpel (fig. 32*i*). See also *Achene, Capsule, Nut.*

Gamopetalous With a corolla of one piece, the petals united, at least at the base. See also *Polypetalous.*

Genotype The genetic constitution of an organism. See also *Phenotype.*

Genus The taxonomic group between family and species. Plural *Genera.*

Gills Plates on the underside of the cap in some species of fungi (fig. 15*a*).

Glabrous Without hairs.

Glands Secreting organs (fig. 24).

Glochid A minute barbed spine or bristle, often in tufts, as seen in many cacti.

Gymnosperms Plant group in which seeds are not enclosed in an ovary (conifers etc.). See also *Angiosperms.*

Gynoecium The female elements collectively, the carpels (fig. 35). See also *Androecium.*

Habit Characteristic growth form of an organism.

Hyaline Thin and translucent (fig. 29).

Hypogynous With sepals, petals, and stamens attached to the receptacle below the ovary. See also *Epigynous, Perigynous.*

Imperfect flower Lacking either stamens or carpels. See also *Perfect flower.*

Indehiscent See *Dehiscence.*

Inferior Beneath or below, as an ovary that appears below the calyx. See also *Superior.*

Inflated Appearing blown up, bladder-like (fig. 42).

Inflorescence A flower cluster with a definite arrangement of flowers.

Irregular flower See *Zygomorphic.*

Keel The two lower united petals of a papilionaceous (pea-type) flower (fig. 41).

Lamina The blade or expanded portion of a leaf.

Leaflet One unit of a compound leaf (fig. 16*d*).

Leaf scar Mark left on site from which a leaf has fallen (fig. 26). See also *Bundle scar.*

Lenticel Small spongy openings in stems and other plant parts in surrounding impermeable tissues, allowing an interchange of gases between internal tissues and the atmosphere (fig. 26).

Linear Long and narrow with margins parallel or nearly so, as in grass leaves.

Monocotyledon One of the two classes of angiosperms. Plants in this group have embryos with one cotyledon. See also *Cotyledon, Dicotyledon.*

Monoecious Having staminate (male) and pistillate (female) flowers borne together on individual plants. See also *Dioecious.*

Mucro A short spur or spiny tip (fig. 19*f*).

Nectary A nectar-secreting gland, often formed as a pit, protuberance or scale (fig. 45).

Node Point on a stem where one or more leaves are attached.

Nut One-celled and one-seeded indehiscent hard-coated fruit (fig. 32*j*). See also *Achene, Capsule, Follicle.*

Ontogeny The life-history of an individual organism.

Opposite Buds or leaves occurring on each side of an axis in pairs at nodes.

Ovary The ovule-bearing part of a carpel or a gynoecium composed of fused carpels (fig. 35). The ovary becomes the fruit after the fertilization and maturation of the ovules.

Ovule The organ, contained in the ovary, which after fertilization becomes the seed (fig. 35).

Palmate Divided in a hand-like fashion (fig. 16*b*)

Papillae Minute pimple-like protuberances (fig. 33*d*).

Pappus Tufts of hairs, bristles or scales, on the fruits (achenes) of composites (Asteraceae or Compositae).

Pedicel The stalk of an individual flower in a cluster.

Peduncle The stalk of an inflorescence.

Perfect flower Having both stamens and carpels. See also *Imperfect flower.*

Perianth The corolla and calyx together.

Perigynous With petals and stamens arising from the margin of a cup-shaped extension of the receptacle. Often apparently attached to the ovary. See also *Epigynous, Hypogynous.*

Petal One of the units of the corolla.

Petaloid Resembling a petal (fig. 40).

Petiole Leaf stalk.

Phenotype The appearance of an organism due to interaction between its genetic constitution (genotype) and the environment. See also *Genotype.*

Phyllary A bract, especially of the inflorescence of the composites.

Pinnate A compound leaf with leaflets placed on each side of the rachis (fig. 16*d*).

Pistil An organ consisting of stigma, style (where

present) and ovary; a pistil may be of one carpel or several fused together (fig. 35).

Pollen Grains carrying the male reproductive element produced in the anthers.

Polypetalous With a corolla of separate petals. See also *Gamopetalous*.

Pome Simple fleshy fruit found only in one subfamily of the Rosaceae (apples, pears, quinces etc.). See also *Drupe, Berry*.

Pubescent Covered with short soft hairs; downy.

Rachis Axis; in compound leaves the extension of the petiole corresponding to the midrib of the entire leaf.

Radially symmetrical See *Actinomorphic*.

Ray florets The zygomorphic flattened flowers surrounding the *Disc florets* in most Asteraceae (aster family or Compositae) (fig. 37).

Receptacle The part of the axis of the flower stalk that bears the floral organs (fig. 35).

Reflexed Abruptly bent downward or backward.

Regular flower See *Actinomorphic*.

Revolute With margin rolled toward the lower side (fig. 19b).

Rosette Leaves radiating from a crown or centre.

Rugose Used of a wrinkled leaf-surface with the venation seemingly impressed (fig. 20c).

Scarious Applied to leaflike parts or bracts lacking green that are thin, dry, and more or less transparent.

Seed The ripened ovule (fig. 33).

Sepal A unit of the calyx (fig. 35).

Serrate Used of a leaf margin with forward-pointing saw teeth (fig. 19f).

Sessile Lacking a stalk.

Sinuate See *Undulate*.

Spathe valves One or more scarious bracts enclosing a developing inflorescence or flower.

Species A taxonomic category below genus. The primary unit of classification for plants and animals.

Stamen The unit of the androecium; comprised of anther and filament, though sometimes the latter is lacking (fig. 35).

Staminate Male; having stamens and no carpels.

Staminode A sterile stamen or a structure resembling a stamen carried in the staminal part of a flower.

Standard The upper petal of a papilionaceous (pea-type) flower (fig. 41c); the usually erect unit of the inner series of the perianth of an iridaceous (iris-type) flower (fig. 40).

Stigma The part of the carpel that receives the pollen (fig. 35).

Stigmatic Of the stigma.

Stipule A basal appendage of a petiole (fig. 18).

Style More or less elongated tissue connecting stigma and ovary (fig. 35). Sometimes absent.

Superior An ovary free and separate from the calyx.

Taxon Any one of the categories such as family, genus, species etc. into which organisms are classified (plural *Taxa*).

Taxonomy The science of the classification of organisms. Hence *Taxonomist*.

Tepal A unit of those perianths that are not clearly differentiated into corolla and calyx.

Trichome An outgrowth of the epidermis such as a hair, scale or water vesicle (fig. 24).

Tuber Short, swollen, underground stem functioning as a storage organ, as in potato (fig. 29d).

Tubercle A rounded protruding body as in some cacti (fig. 25).

Tunic The loose, often fibrous membrane about a corm or bulb.

Undulate A leaf or petal margin waved up and down at right angles to the body of the organ (fig. 19d); contrasting with *Sinuate* where movement is in the same plane as the rest of the leaf, petal etc. – towards and away from a midrib (fig. 19c).

Vascular Used of plant tissue consisting of or giving rise to conducting tissue.

Venation The arrangement of veins.

Versatile Attached near the middle and usually moving freely, as with mode of attachment to filament.

Whorl A circle of leaves or flower parts.

Wings Lateral petals of a papilionaceous (pea-type) flower (fig. 41c).

Zygomorphic A flower divisible into matching halves along one plane only. Used of a bilaterally symmetrical or irregular flower (fig. 36a, b, c, g).

Selected bibliography

ARBER, A. *Herbals: Their Origin and Evolution: a chapter in the history of botany, 1470-1670.* Cambridge University Press, 1938

BLUNT, WILFRID *The Art of Botanical Illustration* New Naturalist series, 4th edn, Collins, London, 1967

BLUNT, WILFRID & RAPHAEL, S. *The Illustrated Herbal* Frances Lincoln, London, and State Mutual Book, New York, 1979

CALMANN, GERTA *Ehret: Flower Painter Extraordinary* Phaidon Press, Oxford, and New York Graphic, New York, 1977

Curtis's Botanical Magazine 1787-; currently published by the Bentham-Moxon Trust, Royal Botanic Gardens, Kew in assoc. with Curwen Books, London

DESMOND, R. *Dictionary of British and Irish Botanists and Horticulturists, including plant collectors and botanical artists* Taylor & Francis, London, and Rowman & Littlefield, Totowa, NJ, 1977

DUNTHORNE, G. *Flower and fruit prints of the 18th and early 19th centuries* Dulau, London, 1938. Facs. edn Da Capo Press, New York, 1975

HUBBARD, C. E. *Grasses* Penguin, London, 1959

HULTON, P. & SMITH, L. *Flowers in Art from East and West* British Museum Publications, London, 1979

Hunt Institute for Botanical Documentation *Catalogue of the ... International Exhibition of Botanical Art and Illustration* Carnegie Mellon University, Pittsburgh, 1964-

Index Londinensis to illustrations of flowering plants, ferns and fern allies ... from botanical and horticultural publications of the XVIIIth and XIXth centuries [to 1920]. Prepared under the auspices of the Royal Horticultural Society at the Royal Botanic Gardens, Kew, by O. Stapf. Clarendon Press, Oxford, 1929-31. Supplement for 1921-35 by W. C. Wordsell, Oxford, 1941. Lubrecht & Cramer, Monticello, NY

ISAACSON, R. T. *Flowering Plant Index of illustration and information.* Sponsored by The Garden Center of Greater Cleveland. G.K. Hall, Boston, Mass. 1979

KING, RONALD *Botanical Illustration* Ash & Grant, London, 1978; Potter, New York, 1979 (dist. by Crown)

LAWRENCE, GEORGE H. M. *Introduction to Plant Taxonomy* Collier-Macmillan, London, 1955

LAWRENCE, GEORGE H. M. *Taxonomy of Vascular Plants* Macmillan, New York, 1955

LOWSON; J. M. *Textbook of Botany* 15th edn E. W. Simon *et al,* University Tutorial Press, Cambridge

NISSEN, C. *Die botanische Buchillustration: ihre Geschichte und Bibliographie* [*Botanical book-illustration: its history and bibliography*] Hiersemann, Stuttgart, 1951-66

'Printing' by Helen Hemingway Benton in *The New Encyclopaedia Britannica* (vol. 14) 1975

RAVEN, PETER with RAY EVERT & HELENA CURTIS *Biology of Plants* 3rd edn Worth Publishers, New York, 1981 (dist. by European Book Service, Weest, Netherlands)

RIX, MARTYN *The Art of the Botanist* Lutterworth, Guildford & London, 1981; Overlook, New York, as *The Art of the Plant World*

SITWELL, SACHEVERELL & BLUNT, WILFRID *Great Flower Books 1700-1900* Collins, London, 1956

STEARN, WILLIAM T. *The Australian Flower Paintings of Ferdinand Bauer* Basilisk Press, London, 1976

STEINBERG, S. H. *Five Hundred Years of Printing* revised edn Penguin, London and New York, 1979

A Vision of Eden: the life and work of Marianne North abridged text by Graham Bateman; Webb & Bower, Exeter, 1980 in collaboration with The Royal Botanic Gardens, Kew; Rhinehart & Winston, New York

In preparation

CARR, D. J. (ed) *Sydney Parkinson, artist of Cook's 'Endeavour' Voyage* Australian National University Press, Canberra

Index

Italic numbers indicate illustrations. Plants are entered under their scientific names, except where common names alone have been used in the text. The *Selected Bibliography* (p. 149) is not indexed.

Accuracy, 26
Acrylics, 127-39; additives, 128, 129; brushes, 128; colour mixing, 132-4, *133*; colour record, 131-2; drawing-board, 129; first trial subject, 134, 137-8, *136*; palettes, 129; pastel shades, 131-2; pencils, 129; pigments, 127-8; plant subject, 138-9, *136*; priming, 130-1, *130*; retardant, 129; supports, 129; techniques, 133-9; varnishing, 128; water-jar, 129
Adams, Lee, 19
Alkyd resin paints, 10, 11
Analysis of subject, 34-6
Angiosperms, 57
Art of Botanical Illustration, The, 20
Ascarina lucida, 74

Basic sketch, 33-6, *35*
Bateman, James, 14
Bauer, Ferdinand L., 13, *108*
Bauer, Franz, 13, 14, *15*, *107*
Bellini, Giovanni, 12
Bewick, Thomas, 17
Bignonia hybrid, 97, *96*
Biology of Plants, 25, 52, 58
Blunt, Wilfrid, 7, 19, 20
Body-colour, *see* Water-colour, opaque (gouache)
Botanical Magazine, 13
Brunfels, Otto, 12
Brushes, 100-1, 128
Buds, 48, *48*
Bulbs, 45, *46*

Cactus structure, 43, *43*
Calculator, 24, 143
Camera, 23-4, 140, 141
Campsis radicans, 105
Capitulum, 52-5, *53, 54*
Caspari, Claus, 20
Codex Vindobonensis, 98
Colour mixing, *see* Acrylics; Water-colour
Conservation (plant), 11, 31

Continuous tone, *see* Pencil
Convallaria majalis, 12
Corms, 45
Craft knife (mat knife), 24, 65
Crayon, 10
Crocus baytopiorum, 18
Curtis, Helena, 58
Curtis, William, 13

De Materia Medica, Dioscorides, 98
Dissecting needles, 24, 28
Dissection, 28, 87-91
Diverse plant structures, 33
Dividers, 24; proportional, 24
Dowden, Anne Ophelia, 19, *19*
Drake, Miss, 14
Drawing-boards, 22, 102, 129
Drawing-stand, 22, *22*
Dry-bush, 112-13, *113*
Dry point, 10
Duo-tone, 64
Dürer, Albrecht, 9, 12, *10*

Egg tempera, 10
Ehret, Georg Dionysius, 13, *13*
Emery paper, 66
Engraving: copper, 10, 12; lead, 10; steel, 10; wood, 10, 16-17
Epilobium latifolium, 85, 86
Equipment, basic, 21-4; specialized – under relevant chapter heads
Erasers, 66-7; in use, 67, 77, 82
Etching, 10
Evert, Ray, 58

Fawcett, Priscilla, 19
Feather, 24, 67
Fitch, John Nugent, 16
Fitch, Walter Hood, 16, 40, 58, *16*
Five hundred Years of Printing, 144
Fixatives, 64
Flindersia australis, 108
Flowers: actinomorphic, 52-5, *53, 55*; dissection, 87-91, *89*; parts, 52-63,

52, *61*; zygomorphic, 52, 56-9, *53, 56, 57, 58*
Fruits, 48-50, *49*
Fuchs, Leonard, 12

Gamopetaly, 57
Gardeners' Chronicle, The, 40, 58
Gauci, 14
Goethe, 11
Gouache, *see* Water-colour, opaque (body-colour)
Grasses, 63
Grierson, Mary, 19, *18*
Growth-phase, 27
Gummed paper strip, 102
Gymnosperms, 59

Hand-lens, 23, 87
Hatching, *see* Ink, Pencil, Scraper board
Herbarium specimens, 30-2
Herbarum Vivae Eicones, 12
Hubbard, Charles Edward, 63
Hunt Institute for Botanical Documentation, 10, 20

Iberis semperflorens, 13
Inflation, 57
Ink, 78-91; erasers, 82; errors, 82, 85, 87, *83*; hatching, 84-5, *85*; line, 83-4, *80, 81, 84*; paper, 81-2; reduction, 78, 144-5, *84*; stipple, 84-5, *85*; studies, 84-7, *80, 86*

Krateuas, 12, 98

Lathyrus latifolius, 14
Lawrence, George H. M., 9
Leaves, 36-42; arrangements, 42; forms, 37-8, *37*; margins, 38, *39*; modelling, 39, *39*; outlines, 37-8, *37*; in perspective, 40, *40*; posture, 41, *42* venation, 39-40, *39*; venation in water-colour, 114, 117, 118, *113*
Leonardo da Vinci, 12
Les Roses, 13
Lettering, 145
Letterpress, 64
Lighting, 21, 28-9
Line, *see* Ink, Pencil
Line, subjective or implied, 69-70
Linnaeus, 12-13, 26
Lino cuts, 10
Lithography, 10, 14, 16

Magnolia grandiflora, 19

Measurements, 34-5, 36, 142-3
Meyer, Albrecht, 12
Microscope, dissecting, 23, 28
Models, plant, 27-8; handling, 28-9; storage, 29-30

Nectaries, 63, *63*
New Encyclopaedia Brittanica, The, 144
North, Marianne, 19

Oils, 10, 98
Orchidaceae of Mexico and Guatemala, 14
Orchids, 57-9, *58*
Ornamentation (of stems and branches), 43-5, *44, 45*

Paeonia suffruticosa, 106
Palettes: for water-colours, 102; for acrylics, 129
Papaver cultivar, poppies, 125-6, *135*
Paper: for acrylics, 129; for ink, 81-2; for pencil, 66; stretching, 103-4, *103*; for water-colour, 101-2
Parkinson, Sydney, 19, *17*
Pencils: aquarelle, 10; colour, 10; extender for, 65, *65*; for use with ink, 83; for use with scraper board, 92-3; for use with water-colour, 103; grades, 64; sharpening, 65-6, *65*
Pencil techniques, 67-77; continuous tone, 72-7, *frontispiece, 73, 74, 75, 76*; doodling, 67-8, *68*; hatching, 70-2, *71*; line, 67-70, *69*; on textured paper, 66, *66*; white line, 77, *75, 76, 77*
Pens, 78-80; and wash, 10; marks, 80, 83-5, *80*
Perspective, 25, 35
Phenotypic variation, 27
Photography, 9, 17, 140-3
Pisanello, 12
Plant names (scientific versus vernacular), 26
Plant-stand, 23, *23*
Pliny the Elder, 12, 98
Polypetaly, 57
Posture, plant, 41, *41*
Presentation of work, 145
Pricker, 24
Proserpina, 11, 59
Pteris serrulata, 17

Ranunculus bulbosus, 79; *R. repens*, creeping buttercup, *frontispiece*
Raven, Peter H., 58

Redouté, Pierre-Joseph, 13, *14, 106*
Reduction, 78, 144, *84*
Register marks, 144
Rhododendron campylogynum, 118
Rieful, Carlos, 20
Roots, 46-8, *47*
Rosa canina, dog rose, *69*
Ross-Craig, Stella, 19, *79*
Ruskin, John, 11

Scale, 34, 89-90, 145
Scalpel, 24, 28
Scanning electron microscope, 50
Scraper board, 92-7; cutting, 95-7;
    doodling, 93, *93*; hatching, 93-4, 97,
    93; leaf study, 94-7, *95*; priming
    white board, 94; plant study, 97, *96*;
    tone, 93-4, *93, 95, 96*; tools, 92, *92*;
    transferring design, 94-5
Seat, 22
Seeds, 50-1, *50*; lighting, 51, *51*
Selenicereus hamatus, 16
Serigraphs, 10
Sexual structures and expression, 59-
    62, *61*
Solanum macrocarpon, 13
Spaëndonck, Gerard van, 13, *13, 105*
Steinberg, S. H., 144
Stems, 43-5, *44, 45*; shading, 85, *85, 87*
Stereocaulon sp., 73-7, *73*
Stipple, *see* Ink
Stipules, 38, *38*
Stones, Margaret, 19
Storage of plant material, 29-30
Storage organs, 45, *46*
Strelitzia reginae, 107

Tape, invisible mending, 24
Taraxacum officinale, dandelion, 138-9,
    136
Taxonomy of Vascular Plants, 9
Thutmose III, 12
Tone (shading), 44, 45, *45*; acrylics, 132,
    134, 137-9, *136*; ink, 47-8, 78, 83,
    84-5, 91, *47, 79, 80, 85, 86, 87, 89,*

91; pencil, 67-9, 70-7, *frontispiece, 68,
    69, 71, 72, 73, 74, 75, 76, 77*; scraper
    board, 92, 93, 94, 97, *93, 95, 96*;
    water-colour, 111-13, 119-23, 125-
    6, *113, 118, 135*
Tone values, 25, 121-2, *25*
Trichomes, 42-3, *42*
Tropaeolum majus, nasturtium, 121-3,
    117
Tubers, 45

Venation, 39-40, *39*; in water-colour,
    114, *113, 117, 118*
Voucher specimens, 30, 143

Water-colour, opaque (gouache or
    body-colour), 98-9, 124-6, *135*;
    technique, 124-6
Water-colour, transparent, 98-124;
    brushes, 100-1; colour layout, 114-
    16, *115*; colour mixing, 25, 111, 116;
    dry-brush, 112-13, *113*; erasure,
    123-4, first plant subject, 119-21,
    118; gradated wash, 111-12, *111*;
    modifying colours, 116, 119, *120*;
    pans, 99; paper, 101-2; pigments, 99-
    100; second plant subject, 121-3, *118*;
    shadow colour, 116; stretching paper
    for, 103-4, *103*; techniques, 103-23,
    110, 111, 113, 114; tone, 111-12,
    121-2, *111*; for translucency, 122-3,
    117; tubes, 99; as used for venation,
    114, *113*; wash, 109-11, *110*; white
    areas, 113-14, *114*; white flowers,
    124
Water-jar, 102
Weiditz, Hans, 12, *12*
White line, *see* Pencil
Withers, Mrs, 14
Woodcuts, 10, 12, *12*
Working surface, 22
Work space, 21

Zahn, Martin, 20